LITTLE TICH

LITTLE TICH

Giant of the Music Hall

Mary Tich and Richard Findlater

With a Foreword by
JACQUES TATI

ELM TREE BOOKS

LONDON

First published in Great Britain 1979
by Elm Tree Books/Hamish Hamilton Ltd
Garden House 57–59 Long Acre London WC2E 9JZ

Published in the United States of America by Elm Tree Books
in association with David & Charles Inc,
North Pomfret, Vermont, 05053, USA

British Library Cataloguing in Publication Data
Tich, Mary
    Little Tich.
    1. Little Tich   2. Comedians, English – Biography
    I. Title   II. Findlater, Richard
    792. 7'028'0924   PN2598.L/   78–41224
    ISBN 0-241-10174-3

Printed in Great Britain by
Bristol Typesetting Co. Ltd, Barton Manor, Bristol

Little Tich was a really great comedian, a star of the first magnitude for ever twinkling.

J. B. Priestley, *Particular Pleasures*, 1975

Genius is not too big a word to use of Little Tich. He has that strange and incalculable endowment, that thing which you cannot acquire and to which all else is added.

Manchester Guardian, 1928

Little Tich was a wonderful artist, with a deep rich voice and with great command. He presented a creature partly human, partly animal. His huge feet belonged to another world, not quite human. Sometimes they embarrassed him, sometimes they applauded him, and he could stand up on them elevated into a victory. This was an extremely *bizarre* art, but he was accepted by the rather simple music hall audience as being no more than a trifle odd. Little Tich was *enormous*.

Sir Ralph Richardson, in a letter, 1978

Little Tich was one of the most intelligent men who ever trafficked in absurdity, and it would be doing him a great injustice to assume that his funniness was due only to his stature. Whatever his build, he could not have escaped being a great comedian, for he was born with all the attributes of comic genius . . .

Sir Louis Ferguson, *Old Time Music Hall Comedians*, 1949

Like Nellie Wallace, another genius of the halls who was a superb dancer, he was an embodiment of the London backstreets, but also resembled a drawing by Callot, or one of the demons of Hieronymus Bosch.

Sacheverell Sitwell, *Sunday Times*, 1951

A*

CONTENTS

ILLUSTRATIONS

FOREWORD

Little Tich was professor to a great number of comics, and as one knows that few students in a class respect the teachings of their master, it is not surprising that a certain self-interested indifference marked the enforced retirement of this great teacher.

To begin with, one important factor must be underlined : there is a great deal of difference between the Eccentric, a category into which Little Tich fitted, and the clown who is still known today as the Auguste. Because of his intelligence, the Eccentric is a solitary and needs no one to assert himself. He is simultaneously author/actor and his own motivator or 'faire valoir'. The Eccentric draws energy for his own movements from the action itself, while the clown needs a partner so as to recharge his forces.

Little Tich could have spent his whole life performing the same act. He disapproved of this facility and spent his time bringing into question and reconsidering his comic action. There are a few, and I am one of those few, to have followed this forerunner in the defence of artistic freedom.

The film of his Big Boots act, the only one I know of, remains as a foundation for everything that has been realized in comedy on the screen. My greatest regret is not to have seen the numerous innovations that Little Tich could have brought to filming, with his parodies of formal receptions, of Belle Otéro, of Loie Fuller, and so many more. Film enthusiasts today could then understand that, without Little Tich, the comic film would never have attained its degree of intelligence and that this is owed to him, the giant of creation.

JACQUES TATI

LITTLE TICH

PART ONE

1

TICH IN ACTION

There is no reason why such names as Tich, Leno and Marie
Lloyd should be forgotten any more than such names as Salvini,
Bernhardt and Henry Irving.

Naomi Jacob, *Our Marie*, 1952

Nearly a score of turns have come and gone, greeted with varying
degrees of apathy and approval, on the stage of one of the long-
lost Empires of a buried England. It is about 10.15 on a Saturday
night, before the First World War, at the Tivoli, the London
music hall behind the restaurant in the Strand. Indian gods and
goddesses (in their more chaste poses) decorate the walls of this
temple of pleasure. Expectation soars as the moment approaches
for the top of the bill to make his entrance. An electric thrill
passes through the audience, packed beneath the baroque opulence
of the boxes, and as the illuminated red numbers change in the
frames on each side of the stage, whose flanking pillars are topped by elephants' heads, the band in the orchestra pit starts up
a catchy tune. People start to clap. The applause rises in a swell
of excitement. It ebbs away; the house holds its breath; a bell
buzzes; the band plays the tune again; the curtains swing up; the
limes focus on the left of the stage; and a little man—a *very* little
man—hurries on at high speed into a noisy gale of welcome,
slides to a halt facing the audience, and receives their homage with
an incomparable mixture of frank delight, elfish dignity and knowing amusement. Little Tich is on.

The Tivoli applause is immediately charged with laughter,
although Tich has not yet said a word or sung a note or done a
thing. There is nothing especially comic about his make-up (reddened nose and chin) or his costume: he is wearing a somewhat
battered gibus, a very short jacket in large black-and-white checks,
and baggy trousers, but this outfit—though scarcely naturalistic—
is restrained when compared with the grotesque gear of some of
his predecessors on the bill. This man is wearing something much
more important, a mischievous, sweet, immensely infectious grin,

3

as he eyes the house with a conspiratorial relish that invites them all to share the joke that he soon can scarcely contain, shaking with suppressed laughter, spluttering asides that he chokes on guiltily, swivelling a fearful eye at the boxes that suggests a pilferer caught in the act—till the smile comes back, as it always shines through all Tich's stage adversities, blandly menacing but irresistibly winning.

Why is the house laughing before Little Tich has apparently started? Because of his reputation—he has been a bill-topping byword since 1890. Because he is advertised (in succession to Dan Leno) as The Funniest Man on Earth. Because he is uncommonly short. Because they have been *waiting* to laugh. And because a lot of them have had a lot to drink. There is another reason: contrary to appearances, he *has* already started working. As soon as he came on the stage he connected with the emotional voltage in the auditorium, concentrated it and somehow intensified it, by the power that great performers often apply, that lucky audiences sometimes experience, and that nobody has ever satisfactorily explained; which is why people still call it magic. He has galvanized the Tivoli audience with a two-way charge of affection and sympathy that, if the gods are willing, and if neither his prodigious vitality nor his technical expertise nor his artist's instinct fails, will carry him through his turn. And it all scarcely takes a minute: Little Tich can't afford more, because he has barely fifteen minutes at most, although he is topping the Tivoli bill and is the highest paid artist of his kind in the world. *Of his kind?* There's nobody quite like him on the halls.

During his first number Tich shows why he is still a popular idol after twenty years: not so much in the song itself or in the patter, but rather in the comic intensity of his characterization, the finesse of his 'business', the impish, quicksilver energy with which he darts around the stage, as if continually improvising, as if *at play*. When he starts off he has the air of a man who has just had an exceptionally good dinner, topped off by a fine brandy and a splendid cigar. He looks as if he has every reason to feel pleased with himself. Then everything begins to go wrong. Things revolt against him. Twirling his cane, like a would-be swell, he manages to poke himself in the eye with it. Recovering quickly, with the same ineffable smile that he wore at his entrance, he shortly afterwards drops it on the stage—and pounces on it, snatching it up as if it were a naughty child. Then his hat falls

4

off, and—taking a life of its own—refuses to be recaptured. His shoes, too, rebel against him; they trip him up and behave very oddly. At first he shrugs his shoulders at these misfortunes, and ignores them: the effects of the dinner and the cigar have not yet worn off. But gradually his morale is affected. He tries to quell the rebellious elements, *tame* them, plead with them. He chases his hat unavailing around the stage, smiling apologetically at the audience, until he suddenly hits on the idea of carrying out an encircling movement, which he does with ostentatious insouciance, and claps the hat back on his head. But a moment later, when he drops both the hat and the cane, he is plunged into a terrible dilemma: *which one will he pick up first?* He starts to move towards the cane, but breaks off half-way to head for the hat. He wavers again, and again, and again, miraculously taking the audience with him in what he calls 'the business of being undecided', but never stretching out the game for a moment too long. Suddenly his cane begins to slip down a hole in the stage, drilled for that purpose, and he goes with it, 'his eyes glaring, his face a study in epileptic dismay, his mouth a horrified little jam-puff,' carrying on an imaginary struggle with the demons below.

In the course of his turn Little Tich goes off three times to the quick-change booth in the wings, returning as a waiter and a gamekeeper, grotesques in extravagant make-up and costume who are nevertheless imbued with instantly recognizable humanity, miniatures brought to life in a song and patter for their few minutes on the stage with a hundred comic touches, movements, vocal inflections. Off he goes after the last song, to be recalled by furious applause, and whistles, and shouts of 'Boots!' 'Big Boots!' Obediently, after some byplay of protest, he kneels down on the stage. While the band repeats that catchy little piece of music over and over again, out of the wings towards him come hurtling two large, flat, heavy, narrow clogs, each twenty-eight inches long, more than half Tich's height. These are the Big Boots, and as each arrives it is greeted with an enthusiastic round of applause. Slowly, carefully, spinning out the ritual, Little Tich puts the boots on, chuckling obscurely to himself, pausing to struggle with a supposedly refractory lace or to tap out a syncopated coda to the never-ending music with one clog before he tries it for size. At last they are both on, and he begins his grotesque 'dance', a showpiece of acrobatic strength and skill as well as comic timing,

5

slapping his feet down so vigorously to the rhythm that the dust rises in clouds. When his hat falls off, he leans forward at a perilously acute angle and scoops it up without bending his knees. He slides across the boards, doing the splits fast or slow. He falls over on his nose, with his feet still flat on the floor, then turns his face round and up to the audience to show that he's laughing. He sits down, bringing his legs together so that his face is hidden from the stalls by the boots. Then he slowly opens his legs again, beams out coyly at the audience, snaps the boots shut and cries out with pain ('Oo-er!') as if his fingers had somehow got caught between. He leans forward to take a bow, so very far forward that it seems certain he will topple over into the orchestra pit; he doesn't, but he hits his forehead on the stage in a near-horizontal position, then raises himself to the upright position again, straight-legged, with magical rapidity. Then, finally, he reaches the longed-for consummation of the 'dance'. Slowly, winking knowingly at the house as if he were inviting them to share in another of his minor debacles, Little Tich rises up on the toes of his elongated wooden feet. Defying the laws of gravity, the manikin has become—for a moment of delicate balance—a giant nearly seven feet tall.

In a minute the dance is over. To tumultuous applause from the Tivoli audience Little Tich goes off; the red numbers change in the proscenium frames; a bell buzzes; the conductor strikes up a new signature tune. Not long afterwards, a serious, dandyish, dignified little man slips quickly out of the stage door, followed by his driver, into his waiting limousine, where he occupies a special high seat in the back. Mr Harry Relph is resuming his private life, a life that he kept rigidly separate from his professional career, and about which he maintained a secrecy that has persisted since his death fifty years ago.

Some attentive readers of the trade press may have known that Tich had unusual off-stage hobbies. He was a skilful, assiduous artist in oils, water colour and black-and-white; he enjoyed photography; he read widely, in religion, philosophy and literature. ('A knowledge of the best in literature,' he said, 'can help even a comedian'); he loved to play the 'cello (as well as billiards, chess and golf) and he both composed and arranged music for his act; he was a versatile linguist. He had other hobbies, too. But a great deal of his private life must remain today as much of a mystery as his comic genius. This word 'genius' is, of course, a dangerously

6

devalued superlative, wrecked by generations of show business publicists; but it was used frequently in Tich's lifetime by discriminating observers, and we use it advisedly here because (so it appears to us) no other term will quite do.

Our introductory sketch above of Harry Relph as Little Tich can do little more than suggest his impact upon a London audience in his prime; and it risks giving the impression that the Big Boots Dance was the apotheosis of his art. (In fact, he grew to hate it. It was disproportionately gruelling. He discarded it in the last thirteen years of his life, however hungrily audiences longed to see it again. And he surpassed it in his maturing achievements.) But Tich needs an introduction, because he has been oddly undervalued and overlooked. In spite of the difficulties of documenting the *personal* life of so private, reticent and modest a man as Harry Relph, who left behind him so little evidence in the shape of letters or journals; and in spite of the insuperable problems of evoking in print the *professional* mastery of a virtuoso performer whose funniness and fantasy died with him; yet we believe that it is worth while attempting to recreate the two lives of Little Tich in a book. Not only because of the filial piety of one author of this book; but also because he was one of the great artists of European music hall in a great European tradition (though it took the Americans to 'discover' him); and because it seems absurd that while scores of middling 'straight' talents have been celebrated by biographies in the past half-century, there is nothing outside newspaper and periodical reviews but a Joe Miller-ish paperback of 1911 (which he virtually disowned; it was ghosted by Sax Rohmer before he discovered Fu Manchu) and a few scattered paragraphs in reminiscences to record the work of a man honoured by the Sitwells and the Guitrys, Coquelin and Tati, Sarcey and Agate, Toulouse-Lautrec and Nijinsky, Priestley and Beerbohm. And the reasons for their admiration are not apparent in the surviving recordings of Tich's songs, or in the scrap of spotty, flickering film, nearly eighty years old, preserved by the British Film Institute and elsewhere. There is, it seems to us, another reason for trying to tell Harry Relph's story: which is, that it is the story—sad, funny and mysterious by turn—of an extraordinary man in an extraordinary profession.

Like its subject, this book is of unconventional shape. It is short, although Little Tich's working life—unlike that of so many

British music-hall stars—endured for half a century (ending with his mastery modulated though unimpaired). And it is divided into two sections: about Little Tich the artist, and about Harry Relph the man. That is the way he divided his life himself, with exceptional care and precision. A conventional, chronological narrative, with a detailed survey of theatrical and domestic events, is beyond our powers. With the aid of Harry Relph's surviving professional scrapbooks, the recollections of his family, and the fragments we have scraped together from sources indicated where possible in the text and gratefully acknowledged in our Postscript, we have told his story as best we can—in the service of theatrical history, and for the entertainment of the general reader to whom Little Tich is now, at best, a name.

2

THE SIXTEENTH CHILD

Quite a lot of folks seem to think a comedian just happens. *They have an idea that he grows one night, like a mushroom—or a toadstool. I know there are folks who think that about me.*

Little Tich

It was out of the British public-house that the British music hall grew in Victorian times; and it seems felicitously apt that a pub should be the birthplace of one of its greatest stars, Harry Relph, known for most of his life as Little Tich. Yet the inn where he was born on 21 July 1867, and where he spent his first seven years, was not one of those busy urban taverns or 'free and easies' where the age-old arts and crafts of 'variety' performers found a new home a century ago: it was a quiet rural pub in a secluded corner of Kent—the Blacksmith's Arms, Cudham. Even today this tiny hamlet, straggling along the road from Westerham to Orpington, high on a wooded ridge above the meadows below, retains the unmistakeable atmosphere of a village. Officially, Cudham is part of the London borough of Bromley, and commuters' colonies choke the countryside for miles around neighbouring towns and villages. Yet the view from the Blacksmith's Arms —strategically sited about a hundred yards from the church, beside a road junction and the erstwhile forge—looks much as it must have done to Harry Relph a century ago; and the inn itself, from the outside at least, does not appear to have radically changed.

The landlord was Harry's father, Richard Relph, who came from a Kentish family that may be traced back to the beginning of the eighteenth century, and was linked especially with the village of Fawkham, his birthplace, some eighteen miles northeast of Cudham. Richard Relph was one of four brothers said to be closely alike in appearance, all of them tall, swarthy and reputedly handsome, with long black hair. He left home early and worked his way around the countryside as a farm labourer and odd-job man, supplementing his earnings by occasional draw-

9

ing and painting, a talent that he later encouraged in Harry. Richard was a man of parts, and it was not long before he began to climb the social ladder, saving money and multiplying it by skilful horse-trading, investing in land and property. In his midtwenties he settled in Fawkham, acquired the local pub, the Rising Sun (the name, at least, survives) and married a local girl, Sarah Ashenden, by whom he had eight children, born between 1819 and 1835. He became a prosperous man, with a farm, a timber business, a paper mill and woodlands which supplied the timber and pulp for these concerns. Richard's wife died in 1845 at the age of fifty-one. Richard remained at the Rising Sun until all but one of his children had left the fold, giving each a part of his property. But he was plainly a man of exceptional vitality, for about 1851—when he was over sixty—he started to raise a second family. He met a young Irish girl, Mary Moorefield or Morphew, whom he later married; and with her he moved first a few miles away to Crockenhill (where she bore him several children); and then to Cudham, where he bought not only the Blacksmith's Arms but also a farm beside it. (The Rising Sun was taken over by his eldest Fawkham son, Richard.) Richard Relph was respected in the area—as much, no doubt, for his paternal fecundity as for his commercial acumen and skill as a publican. (He was, himself, a strict teetotaller.)

For the landlord of the Blacksmith's Arms there was nothing exceptional about the birth in the summer of 1867. He was accustomed to the anxieties of paternity: Harry was his sixteenth child. But for the Cudham customers Harry's arrival had two unusual aspects. One was his father's age: Richard was seventy-seven, and his wife was thirty-two. The second remarkable fact was the baby's hands: Harry was born with ten fingers, in addition to his thumbs. When the family doctor was consulted, he advised amputation of the extra digits; but Harry's mother adamantly rejected such a surgical solution. It would, she said, be 'butchery'. Mrs Relph's protective attitude is understandable, yet a surgical operation then would have saved her son a great deal of misery and bitterness throughout his adult life, although it would have entailed more than simple amputation. Norman C. Lake, a contemporary specialist on polydactylism, as this deformity is known, writes in *The British Encyclopaedia of Medical Practice* (Vol. 6.):

10

A small non-functioning digit should be removed shortly after birth, but a complete functioning extra digit should probably be left alone, since the only reason for its removal would be a cosmetic one, and many patients who have reached adult life with such a deformity regard it as an asset rather than a disability.

For Harry's parents those extra fingers were an asset, certainly, at the start. Trade boomed at the Blacksmith's Arms, as people came over from Westerham, Orpington and nearby villages to see the baby with ten fingers, two thumbs, and a seventy-seven-year-old father. Harry was shown off proudly by his venerable parent, bounced about on the bar counter as visitors and villagers drank to him and to the landlord (with incidental observations, no doubt, on Mr Relph's philoprogenitive powers and gossip about the real identity of Harry's father). What is more, the baby seemed to like it all. He responded 'comically' to such attentions; and from a very early age he appeared to delight in the sound of music and the sight of dancing—notably, the noisily cheerful knees-ups of the Cockney hop-pickers who came to work every summer in the fields below the Blacksmith's Arms. But as he grew older, Harry became acutely and persistently conscious of his extra digits. To him they were never an 'asset'. He found that his nails never grew longer, and that his palms—unlike everybody else's—never had any lines. Moreover, half of each hand—from the little finger to the centre joint—was slightly webbed, so that the complete conventional use of both hands was severely restricted. Harry could not fully clench his fists, or spreadeagle his fingers, as other boys could. He could not wear gloves, only mittens. His hands looked somewhat clumsy—almost monstrously so, in his own view. With the customary cruel conformism of childhood, his contemporaries helped to make him feel a freak. Harry grew up to hate his hands. Throughout his adult life he found it lacerating if people referred to them in print or in conversation. But it is not true that Harry had two thumbs on each hand, as the French critic-historian Tristan Rémy said; or, as his own early publicity stated, that he had six fingers and a thumb on each hand; or, as Jules Renard believed, that he had seven fingers on his right hand only; or that, as J. B. Priestley, Cicely Courtneidge and others have reported, he had twelve toes. His hands gave him more than enough reason for private bitterness, without having

11

to agonize over his feet, which were, in fact, elegantly tiny, strong and swift ('beautiful', indeed, according to his third wife). Luckily, his thumbs and the first two fingers on each hand were unusually flexible, counterbalancing to some extent the handicapped half. Harry developed, moreover, an unusual strength of will-power, making up for his physical deficiencies. With dogged persistence, and the loving help of his mother, he learned to overcome the problems of writing, drawing, painting and, in later years, playing such instruments as the cello and the saxophone, although he could never span a full octave on the piano. He had, moreover, what turned out to be a prime asset in future life: he was double-jointed.

Harry spent the first seven years of his life in Cudham, and the countryside around it. Although his home was the village pub, and he was born into a big family which must have stretched the few private rooms of the Blacksmith's Arms to bursting-point, he led a somewhat solitary existence. His father was a kindly but remote patriarch, old enough (as Harry was no doubt often reminded by joshing friends) to be his grandfather. His mother, though tender and protective, was a hard-worked housekeeper and publican's wife with a large brood to supervise and a persistent aura of melancholy. Born in Ireland, of Irish-Spanish parentage, Mary Moorefield was an orphan, educated in a Dublin convent, who at fourteen or fifteen came to Fawkham as a nurse-maid-governess: one of the female army of colonial near-serfs who kept English family life going. Our almost complete ignorance of her background is illustrated by our uncertainty about the very spelling of her name. On Harry's birth certificate it is 'Morphew'; on her death certificate it is 'Moorefield'. We have settled for 'Moorefield' on the grounds that in an Irish accent it may well have *sounded* to a rural clerk like 'Morphew', and that at her death Harry is unlikely to have sanctioned a mis-spelling of his mother's name. According to family tradition Mary was a reluctant, and for ten years an unmarried bride. She was remembered as a petite, dark-haired, dark-eyed, rather frail and nervous woman, often found in tears, although Richard Relph was said to be a gentle husband. To have had her first child at sixteen by a man forty-five years her senior, and to spend the next sixteen years—ten of them without the status of wife—in bearing and rearing seven more children while running a village inn, might well be thought sufficient reason for some residual

12

sadness. But there is a theory in the Relph family that Mary was unhappy because it was not Richard Relph with whom she had wanted to live but Will Relph, his youngest son by his first marriage, who was her own age; and that she stayed in love with Will long after she became his father's mistress. On a different level of rumour a story went the rounds in Cudham (it is still remembered today) that Will was the true father of Harry. Harry himself seemed to give no credence to this gossip, but it is scarcely surprising it should have arisen when one considers not only the respective ages at Harry's birth of Richard, Mary and Will but also the fact that Will Relph lived with his father's second family at the Blacksmith's Arms, which he helped to run. What is more, Will—who never married, but is said to have had 'an eye for the girls'—went on living with the family after they left Cudham; he went on living in Mary's house after her husband died; and after her death he lived with her daughter, supported by Harry until he died at the age of eighty-five. Yet however intimate the relationship of Will and Mary may have been, Harry's disabilities may be more credibly ascribed to Richard's age at his birth than (as Cudham villagers put it about) to a heavenly punishment of Mary for extra-marital intercourse.

Will Relph was the only member of the Fawkham-born family with whom Harry had any close contact in his childhood. The other half-brothers and half-sisters, who were in their forties when he was born, seemed to him 'old men and women'—strangers rather than relations, although most of them lived not far away in the same county. Harry knew next to nothing about them, and cared less. The Blacksmith's Arms was full of young people and children; but only two—Bob (born 1865) and Agnes (born 1863) were close to Harry in age. His elder brother and sister, John and Elizabeth (Betsy), were thirteen and fifteen when he was born; and there was a big gap, as measured by childhood values, between Harry and the middle group—Amelia or Millie (born 1857), Georgiana or Georgie (born 1858) and Edwin or Ted (born 1861). Right from the start, Harry felt on his own; that, at least, is how he saw his childhood in retrospect. 'They were not interested in me,' he said of his brothers and sisters at Cudham. 'Agnes was the only one. I was always fond of Agnes.' He was painfully aware in childhood of his physical difference: not only his deformed hands but his excessive weight, for he grew abnormally plump.

To add to his disabilities, Harry suffered an accident and hurt his leg one day on the way to school at Knockholt, a three-mile walk from home. Although in considerable pain he managed to reach his school, and the teacher got the local doctor to treat him. But Harry was then left to walk back three miles to the Blacksmith's Arms, and this 'undid the good' of the treatment and threw the leg out of true. For the rest of his life, Harry's right foot turned slightly inwards. It was a distortion that might mean little or nothing to another kind of child, but to young Harry Relph it probably seemed yet another instance that he was out of favour with the Divine Posture-Maker above. In later life he converted this minor deformity, which was generally assumed to be congenital, into another asset of his public performances: the toes-turned-in attitude is a traditionally clownish stance, good for a laugh, and to make people laugh at him was, after all, Harry's vocation.

Yet it was not only Harry's hands, legs and girth that made him feel set apart from his brothers and sisters (Agnes excepted) and from the other children at Cudham and Knockholt. It was also a difference of taste, temperament and sensibility.

Harry Relph was a clever and alert child who could deploy a winning, puckish charm; but he was also a shy and reticent boy, who grew up into an unusually shy and reticent man. At Cudham, it seems, he had already begun to acquire a protective skin: the foundation of the reserve that characterized his manhood, as a performer who liked to be alone. Early on he showed a talent for painting and drawing, prompted by his father, who gave him his first lessons, and by his mother who helped him to overcome the embarrassments of his hands in dealing with crayons and paints. Before he was five he was encouraged by the customers at the Blacksmith's Arms to draw ships and trains to order. He also found pleasure in watching the entertainers who sometimes turned up at the inn: dancers, singers and conjurors, perhaps, alone on their uppers or with a travelling fair. He liked to sing and dance on his own, copying the acts he had seen, childishly imitative but nimble in spite of his plumpness. His elder brothers would sometimes take him with them to a neighbouring village and egg him on to do his turn. Because he was double-jointed, he could do naturally things that had to be painfully learned, in years of gruelling apprenticeship, by many acrobats' sons and pupils. The experience was not always pleasurable. Harry felt that some

14

people didn't laugh with him but *at* him because of his size, double-jointedness, and, maybe, his hands. Yet without realizing it he was beginning to acquire some of the basic training for his future career. The seeds were sown for the later flowering of Little Tich's gifts of timing, musical sense, impromptu dance and audience control.

These years also planted in him an abhorrence of beer, of pubs and (as he came to understand it) the language that he heard in them: an abhorrence confirmed in his adolescence. One of Harry's keenest pleasures was to get away from the Blacksmith's Arms in the company of his black-and-white fox terrier Potty (short for Pottifer), with whom he would ramble around the woods nearby, or gaze at the animals in his father's farm. On several occasions when Mrs Relph thought he was 'lost', Harry was discovered in the stables with the horses; or asleep in a neighbouring coppice where he had gone to look for rabbits. Like many other sensitive children he often felt more at home with birds and animals than with human beings, even his own flesh and blood. He kept that responsiveness to Nature throughout his life, although he spent little time in the country after his childhood was over. When he was out walking with his infant daughter in his fifties, she recalls, he had only to whistle very softly and sparrows would fly down to settle on his head and arms, even though he carried no food to tempt them. 'Stand quite still', he would tell the little girl, as he held out his hands. 'Don't move. Just watch.' The birds didn't notice those fingers.

When Harry was seven, the life at Cudham came to an end. His father, now eighty-four, decided to retire. The eldest boy, John, had become a soldier; Betsy had married; Millie and Georgie were earning a living; so Richard Relph sold the farm and the Blacksmith's Arms—he kept the pub in the family by selling it to one of the daughters of his first marriage—and went off across Kent with Mary, Will and his younger children to settle in Gravesend, where they took a small rented house near the docks area. (It is not known why he chose Gravesend: perhaps because a leading auctioneer and estate agent there, Charles Relph, was his brother, nephew or cousin.) From a tiny secluded village Harry was plunged into the urban bustle of a crowded port, with 20,000 inhabitants and a big floating population of seamen, soldiers, day trippers and holidaymakers. There were scores of pubs, some with entertainers every night; there

B

was Rosherville, a famous pleasure garden, half a mile away; there were steamers to London every day, in the season; there was a real theatre. There was also, for Harry Relph, a new school.

Harry spent three years at Christ Church School in Gravesend. We know nothing about his life there: the records have disappeared and in later years he never talked about his schooldays except about their end, as follows. When he was ten, the headmaster of Christ Church called on Richard Relph to tell him that there was nothing more he could teach Harry, who had outstripped most of the other boys of his age in the speed of his learning. For a boy so intelligent and industrious he recommended higher education at a different school; or, if Mr Relph did not see his way to that, then he suggested that Harry should be apprenticed to a skilled trade like watchmaking. Mr Relph thanked him for his advice, but said no more on the matter to him—or to Harry. When the school broke up a few days later the headmaster paid tribute to Harry, among other boys, in his speech to the assembly, praising in particular his copper-plate handwriting, of which Harry was especially proud—as any boy with deformed hands would be. Everyone at Christ Church, said the head, would miss Harry Relph; and this brought a round of cheers from the boys. Harry never forgot that speech and that applause. It was one of the happiest memories—indeed, one of the very *few* memories—of his early life that he passed on forty years later to his daughter. He also remembered, with equal vividness, the sequel at home. His father summoned him to the parlour. The eighty-seven-year-old patriarch had news for his ten year-old boy.

'Your mother and I are finding things very hard now. We've a great many expenses, and nothing is coming in now that I've retired. I thought that when I sold up at Cudham everyone would be provided for, but those of you who aren't earning their living yet will have to start now. What money is left, after certain important matters are settled, will be only sufficient for your mother and I to live on. Nothing for you, Harry. I don't know what we're going to do with you, my boy. We certainly can't send you to another school. How will you manage?'

'Never mind me, father,' said Harry. 'I'll be all right, don't worry. I'll be able to look after myself.'

Richard Relph had no choice, perhaps. In the 1870s it was by no means unusual for a working class child, in town or country, to start earning his living before his teens. In some ways
16

Harry Relph had led a comfortable, privileged life compared with, say, Dan Leno, who began *his* career at the age of four, dancing for pennies in other people's pubs. Leno had never gone to school at all. Yet the fact that this story was told and retold by Harry in later years, when he had almost nothing to say about the rest of his first decade, suggests how deeply he had been hurt by this abrupt end to his schooldays and the summary declaration of parental independence. One may see why Little Tich, at the height of his fame, once said: 'I don't recall much of my child-hood. There was nothing in it to remember. It was very lonely. That's all.'

In the days of his fame a party from the village, led by Charlie Wood, landlord of the Blacksmith's Arms for some forty years, used to make an annual expedition to see him in a London music hall. Once, at least, they were asked backstage to see him, after they had stopped him in his tracks by yelling out 'Good Old Cudham' on his entrance. In the Blacksmith's Arms today a photograph of Tich in drag (as a huntswoman) is proudly dis-played, together with a pair of 'big boots' in a glass case (though these are, in fact, far *too* big in foot-size to be his). Yet if Cudham was—and is—proud of Little Tich, Harry Relph did not seem to be proud of Cudham. He apparently never went back there and his children were never shown the Blacksmith's Arms. And he seems to have been proud of nothing about Gravesend except that he got out of it—and that he was applauded by his school on the last day of his education.

3

'NIGGER IMPERSONATOR'

I am an artist and not a phenomenon.

Little Tich

In the first decade of his fame, when Little Tich was questioned about his beginnings, he chose to give the impression that he 'drifted' into his profession, largely because his parents had 'a great number of theatrical friends and acquaintances'. It was 'mainly', he said, through seeing so much of this circle (in which it is hard to believe, considering the Relphs' ages and background) and through their 'influence' that he made his first stage appearance, which, like his earlier visits to Gravesend free-and-easies, was kept a secret from his father and mother. But it did not happen in quite that way. Harry Relph did not 'drift' on to the stage: he pushed himself on to it in early adolescence because he *had* to do it.

When he was told by his father to start fending for himself Harry buckled to and got the kind of job in Gravesend that was open to a boy of his age—like working as a lather boy in a barber's shop. But there were, as he knew, better ways of earning money—like entertaining the customers in pubs. From his days at the Blacksmith's Arms he had somehow acquired an alertness to the expectations of an audience, even the least attentive and orderly sort; and in spite of his reluctance to make an exhibition of himself (in the way he had been put on show as an infant) he nonetheless wanted, needed, to sing, to dance, to charm enough customers sufficiently to make them for a while pay attention to him, and so help him to pay his way, however noisy, boorish, impatient and drunk they might be (he had become used to all that). It wasn't only the money that was important, though that came first. He wanted to be applauded, as he had been, once upon a time, at Cudham; to be loved; to be reassured of his identity—in spite of his difference; to show what he could do.

Among the inns near his home there were several which ran

18

nightly entertainment, both professional and amateur, catering for the crowds of soldiers, sailors, merchant seamen and day trippers from London, as well as the local dockworkers, factory hands and tradesmen. One of Harry's friends had a brother in the entertainment business, and when Harry was about ten the two boys went to see him perform at one of these Gravesend halls.

I heard him sing once, and I marked the applause which followed upon his efforts. From that moment I was ambitious. If he could do this thing, could sing and make people laugh, and reap a reward in the shape of tumultuous cheers and hand-clapping, why could I not do likewise? After that I went whenever I could, night after night I went. It was there that I was first seized with a yearning for such fame as comes to the man who acts . . .

Harry was hooked.

By the age of eleven Harry had acquired a tin whistle, and learned how to play it: 'I used to amuse myself by playing all the jolly and sentimental pantomime songs of the day.' He also made something of a name for himself locally among the neighbours with little eccentric dances of his own devising, executed on the cellar-flaps of shops and public houses on his way to and from work. Fifty years later a contemporary remembered that he and a gang of boys met Harry in the street one day and 'asked him to give us one of his funny dances. It was some time before he did so. One of the boys had a penny. This was offered and Little Tich, accepting it, did his dance on the cellar-flap of Mrs Archer's sweet-shop . . . My recollection was that he resented his dance being called a "funny" dance.' He would. He is also said to have played his tin whistle for people queuing to get into the local theatre, busking for pennies.

Harry Relph made his debut before he was twelve, inadvertently, in a back-street free-and-easy, where playing-time was reserved every night for amateurs and beginners. If the customers liked you, they threw pennies on the stage. If they didn't like you, in the rougher establishments of this kind, they were capable of throwing all sorts of less pleasant things inflicting not only physical but also psychological damage. You could get some nasty knocks, just as nasty as those to which variety troupers have always been exposed on bad nights at bad dates. But whatever the eleven-year-old amateur endured in exposing his childish routine

19

to tired and restless Gravesend boozers, he never talked about these in later years. It was roses all the way, at first, or so he sometimes made it sound.

On that first evening, 'during a lull in the show', the chairman rose to his feet and, apparently without any prior warning or connivance, suggested that little Harry Relph wouldn't mind obliging with his tin whistle. Hardly believing his luck and yet hardly daring to chance it, Harry climbed on to the narrow platform that served as stage and, as he put it, 'turned the tin whistle on full.'

> When I finished, the audience threw coppers to me on the platform, and the landlady asked me to come again. There was about a bob in all thrown at me that night, and I was a bit of a millionaire among the other lads. I was rich. Had struck a gold mine. Went every night, and seldom made less than a bob.

Harry added to his popularity there by dancing; and for months he continued to appear at what he called (after the chairman) 'D'Orville's'—which may have been the Privateer, or the King's Head. He did it for the pennies, a valuable supplement to his tips from the barber's shop. 'I liked it and they liked me. At last I found courage to sing, and I sang.'

Directly opposite 'D'Orville's' was a pub on a much grander scale, the Royal Exchange: in due course, this was Harry Relph's next step up the ladder, made again (by his own account) inadvertently.

> This was an awesome place to me. I revered it. They engaged first-rate talent there—talent that appeared in character dress—and two junks of it at a time. Always had a first-rate company of two artistes—a serio and a gent. Tip-top style, I can tell you. Well, I ventured to go there one night. Was gazing on the talent with admiration, when somebody suggested that our little friend here might be induced to oblige with a song and a dance.

Up Harry climbed, in his muddy street-boots, and made a big hit on the spot. 'Enormous! I was engaged right off.'

> Coppers were thrown more liberally there. I had evidently found a high-class audience. I used to have whatever was thrown to me on the platform; and my salary was sixpence a

week. Besides which the landlady, in consideration of the fact that I was a great attraction, used to give me a small lemonade and a ginger-cake every night.

The proprietor of the Royal Exchange, who was also the chairman, the chucker-out and the head barman, bought Harry his first pair of dancing clogs. The boy became a favourite with the customers, singing as often as thirty times every night, with dancing and whistling as well. It was here that he learned to 'black up', in what he described as 'the blackest of Ethiopian styles'.

'When I started in the business,' said Little Tich, 'people thought you couldn't be funny unless you had a burnt-cork face.' In the 1870s there were some 145 'Negro Delineators' at work on the English stage, listed in the *Era Almanack alone*—soloists, brothers, trios, quartets and troupes; and many more performers on the periphery of show business blacked up to be in the fashion. To pretend to be American came as naturally to aspiring English entertainers of the 1870s who specialized in comic songs as it does to their counterparts of the 1970s who want to perform blues, jazz or country and western numbers. That a Norfolk teenager today should sing in the style of Chuck Berry about American city life is taken for granted; so it was in Harry Relph's day for a Gravesend boy of eleven to cherish, as his party piece, a number about the day that he and the other slaves were freed, down on the old plantation. One main difference between the centuries is that Harry and his contemporaries felt obliged to *look* like negroes, because a black face was still in British show business a standing joke in itself, when it was not an excuse for maudlin sentimentality and canting piety. And these Britons with burnt-cork faces were unvexed by anxiety or guilt about racial discrimination.

According to Harry Reynolds, historian of the 'Nigger Minstrels' (which survived on the stage for nearly a century), 'at one time no variety programme was considered complete without the inclusion of two or three black face acts', a 'chair turn' (like a banjo soloist), a pair of 'Ethiopian duettists', and, perhaps, a troupe of black serenaders. George Mozart, Will Evans, the Great Vance, and Bransby Williams were among leading British entertainers who started their careers by 'working black'. One of the top 'Delineators' of the day was E. W. Mackney (1825-1909),

21

then in his early fifties, a Morpeth-born clog-dancer, fiddler, banjo-player and singer who (in modelling himself on Thomas D. Rice, the original Jim Crow) won a position in public favour comparable to Eugene Stratton's in a later generation (though his act was much broader, less sophisticated, and less romantic). It was a sign of Harry Relph's rapid advance in the business that, in no time at all, he should be dubbed 'The Infant Mackney', eagerly shrilling away coon songs above the beery banter, the clouds of smoke, the occasional eruptions of drunken violence. Songs with verses like this:

> O, lor! gals, I wish I'd lots of money,
> Charleston is a mighty place,
> The folk they are so funny
> And they all are bound to go the whole hog or none.

And like this, from Mackney's greatest hit:

> I wish I was with Nancy
> In a second floor, for ever more
> I'd live and die with Nancy
> In the Strand, in the Strand, in the Strand!

In 1880, when he was twelve, Harry graduated to a real stage in the open-air theatre at Rosherville, the seventeen-acre pleasure gardens—last in the tradition of Vauxhall and Cremorne—that were a holiday resort for generations of Londoners arriving by train or 'penny steamer'. Half a mile from Gravesend, 'the place to spend a happy day'—as it was advertised for years—included such treats as an Antique Windmill, a Great Musical Clock, an Archery and Croquet Lawn, an Aquarium, a Maze, a Fernery, a Bear Pit, and a Baronial Hall. In the 1880 season Rosherville also boasted a Gravesend company of blackface entertainers, described by a local historian of the time, J. R. S. Clifford, as 'a band of minstrel darkies of a superior type'. These superior darkies allowed Harry Relph to join them on the stage and play his tin whistle.

He was still, however, an amateur. The transition to professional status (for so he regarded it) came shortly after his Rosherville appearances. The agent who supplied the Royal Exchange with turns was also the conductor at Barnard's music hall in Chatham—the Tin Can, as it was later known. At that time it was a converted pub, dubbed the Railway Tavern and Hall of

22

Varieties: it was among the first to introduce the twice-nightly system, because Barnard staged one performance for rankers and one for officers. Harry appeared for the Barnard's conductor on his benefit night, and scored a big success—although, in Harry's words, 'the music was rather eccentric'.

I had been in such a big way in the profession that I only had one music book [instead of half a dozen band parts]. When I got on the stage, I found the entire band leaning and craning their necks over each other to get a look at it.

The owner, Lew Barnard—'one of the nicest men I ever played for,' said George Robey years later in *Looking Back on Life*—offered Harry an engagement on the spot, at no less than thirty-five shillings a week. The boy from Cudham was beside himself. 'A real engagement at a real hall! Could ambition wish for more?' he said, sixteen years later. It was from that job at Barnard's that Harry Relph dated his professional career; but although he may have started as 'The Infant Mackney' he soon became known by the nickname he had already acquired in Cudham—Young Tichborne. (It has been said that E. W. Mackney insisted on 'The Infant Mackney' being dropped.)

This name, which was later abbreviated to the soubriquet that made him known to millions, was taken from the most bizarre *cause célèbre* of the age. Edgar Lustgarten described the story of the Tichborne Case as 'incredible if it was true, even yet more incredible if it was false'; and its historian Douglas Woodruff wrote in *The Tichborne Claimant* (1957): 'I cannot improve upon that succinct summary.' We must summarize it here, *en passant*, as it was indeed a part of Harry Relph's life.

In 1854 Roger Tichborne, eldest son of a baronet (the tenth) with a sizeable Hampshire estate, was lost at sea. His mother persistently refused to believe that he was dead, and from 1863—the year after Roger's brother succeeded to the title—she started advertising widely in overseas papers for information about her 'missing' son. A response came, somewhat belatedly, from Wagga Wagga in Australia, where a butcher Thomas Castro claimed that he was the rightful heir to the Tichborne estates. After being acknowledged by Lady Tichborne as her son, the Claimant—as he became known—arrived in England in the year of Harry Relph's birth; and, failing to win over the rest of the family, he brought an ejectment action against the estate's trustees. The ensuing cases broke all legal records and turned the Claimant into a national figure, whether he was identified as a working-class impostor threatening the fabric of landed society or (more widely) as a people's friend fighting for his rights against an Establishment conspiracy. After 103 days the Claimant lost the first trial; he was arrested for perjury; and after a trial of 188 days he was found to be Arthur Orton, born in Wapping, and was sentenced to fourteen years penal servitude. What has all this to do with Harry Relph? Because 'Bullocky' Orton was a monstrously fat man who had doubled his weight in four years to nearly twenty-eight stone when the first trial began in 1871. Overweight people were dubbed for a time 'Tichborne', just as forty years later they were called 'Fatty Arbuckle'. As Harry was unusually stout for his age, people who watched him performing in Cudham used to call out 'Come along, little Tichborne' or 'That's it, young Tichborne, show us what you can do'. The name stuck when he became a pro, and persisted after he had lost his puppy fat, acquiring a cruder irony in the contrast between the size of Harry and the Claimant (though, in fact, Orton's weight plummeted to ten stone in prison.) Harry was not the first performer to be nicknamed after the Claimant—around 1870 J. W. Mann bore the Tichborne label—and for a while Harry was called 'Young Tichborne the second'; but he soon became the only one. Gradually the name of Tichborne lost the 'fat' meaning associated with Arthur Orton. It became identified in the abbreviated form of 'Tich' with Harry Relph; and, thereafter, with anyone small.

Although Harry Relph's first professional year began at Chatham with a bang and thirty-five shillings a week it soon dropped to fifteen shillings and six months with no engagements at all. Harry went back to the barber's shop and any other odd jobs he could find. That was the longest spell of unemployment in his career, but he had many weeks 'out' during his next four years on the tread-mill and training-ground of provincial variety in what were later called the Number Threes and Fours; or, as he put it, 'knocking about in the small halls and free-and-easies'. In those days there were no syndicated tours, with managers signing up performers for months, even years, ahead. As Harry said:

We had to write for an engagement each week, as every hall was owned by a different proprietor, and sometimes it was a case of first come, first served. We had to fight for our experience. It was hard work.

When Harry first left home at the age of thirteen to play in towns far from Gravesend his parents sent his favourite sister Agnes with him as a chaperone. But as it soon became apparent that it was Agnes, rather than Harry, who needed chaperoning, he learned to cope on his own, making long and lonely journeys all over England to pubs and halls with his picco (a simpler version of the piccolo), his clogs, his scanty props and his sheaf of music. It is scarcely surprising if Young Tichborne was often cold, hungry, homesick and very tired in these years of apprenticeship, although he rarely spoke about them in later life. Sometimes, no doubt, he had—like his friend T. E. Dunville—to *walk* from one town to the next. Sometimes he may have felt, as Dunville says in his autobiography, 'very glad to work for one's food and lodging alone'.

The air thick with the fumes of shag-laden pipes; the temperature about 80; the concentrated reek of beer; the raucous calls for fresh supplies; the rattle of pint pots in applause; the oaths and shouts of derision if one failed to please, have left an impression upon my mind that I shall carry with me to the grave.

Harry is said to have slept, often, in 'fourpenny dosshouses'; to have starved; and to have survived by dancing and playing his picco outside pubs and for music hall queues.

The reality of this 'pothouse show business' in the provinces—'the spittoons', as these dates were sometimes derisively called in the trade—is far removed from the romanticized, pasteurized image of early Victorian music halls popularized on television. Sometimes the entertainer had to sing and dance on little more than three planks in a corner of the saloon. Even in the real halls, conditions were grim. In one hall, Harry Relph recalled, eleven men had somehow to make up, dress and undress in a small room at almost the same time. 'I have seen dressing-rooms in which the only furniture for five people was a broken chair, a broken table and a remnant of a broken mirror.' Sometimes there were no dressing-rooms at all: Harry more than once had to

25

change and black up behind a curtain across a corner of a bar, where 'there was standing room for one only. You gave the nod to the pianist, drew the curtain aside and you were on the stage.' One such inn was the Dolphin at Kidderminster, where the 'stage' was about two feet high and three feet long. It was, as Harry remembered it, 'one of those little old-fashioned pubs, low windows, diamond panes, red window curtains'. On the first night of his engagement there he found that some of the sixty-odd customers (a full house) were sitting by the edge of the platform, and their quart pots of beer were ranged along it 'just like footlights'. When Harry began to dance 'the pots flew all over the shop, and I had the stage all to myself the next night'. Harry, who was then seventeen, was paid £2 a week, but he was expected to sleep in ('like a shop assistant', he noted disgustedly) and fourteen shillings were 'docked off the screw' for board and lodging. In such places as the Dolphin he had to sing at least thirty times a night, repeating his repertoire over and over again as new customers came in.

> We had to sing at the beck and call of the landlord, or whomsoever he chose to preside over the concert, and if in the course of the evening people who had come into the room had not heard our songs, we were called upon to do another turn. And this went on throughout the whole time the concert hall was open. We were therefore always at work.

In some places that meant attendance through the day, as well. As T. E. Dunville said, 'You had to be ready to give a song as often as there was anyone in the bar.' Licensing hours, like juvenile labour regulations, were flexible. On market days, especially, the pub might stay open till one or two in the morning, and Harry would have to be there on call till it closed. There were no unions to protect artists against managers or pub-proprietors like the one described by Bransby Williams in his autobiography. Williams had been promised four shillings by a Bishopsgate landlord to deliver three songs, do a stump speech and draw cartoons (part of his early speciality). When he had finished his turn, he was paid two shillings only.

> When I asked why not four, the man called a couple of stage hands and said, 'Here, chuck him out, he's saucy!' And they did, into the dark, back street, props and all.

26

Dates might be cancelled and salaries cut at will. And the boy from Gravesend had sometimes to face the resentment of older and bigger men who felt that youngsters like him, exploited by the managers, were undercutting experienced performers. And he had to be sure that, in spite of his meagre pay, he tipped enough— to the right people. Failure to do so might mean, as T. E. Dunville pointed out, that you might suddenly discover part of your props had got 'mislaid', or your skip 'accidentally' sent back to the railway station. In a music hall proper, if the man who changed the programme cards thought you had given him sixpence too little, 'he would put the next number up almost before you had finished your song, so as to do you out of an encore and "queer" you with the manager as much as possible for not winning enough applause'. It should be noted, however, that Little Tich's memories of the Dolphin, at least, could not have been wholly unhappy. Some fifteen years later, when he appeared in a pantomime at Birmingham, he sent tickets for it to the Dolphin proprietor, Samuel Cookson, and his wife; sent his brougham to meet them at the station; and entertained them to tea before the show.

During his five years in the provinces Harry Relph acquired an agent—or, rather, an agent put him on his books. There is some mystery about this connection, and about the reason that Harry later gave for its termination after three years, when he was sixteen. Without Harry's knowledge, he said, this agent had been selling him to managers as a freak, a six-fingered novelty, rather than as an artist. As soon as Harry discovered this, in Leeds, he bade the man goodbye and handled his own business negotiations and contracts. Yet it seems irrefutably clear that Harry acquiesced in this kind of promotion when he was sixteen, if not earlier, for it featured largely on his professional writing paper in 1883. This was headed:

YOUNG TICHBORNE
Surnamed The Claimant's Bootlace
The Eccentric Little Negro Comedian & Champion
Big Clog Dancer
The Little Licker of the Loose Leg Business
The Wonder of the Age, Having Six Fingers and one Thumb
on each Hand: a Decided Novelty.—*Vide Press*

27

On one side of the sheet ran the vertical inscription: YOUNG TICHBORNE, the Picco Soloist; on the other, YOUNG TICH-BORNE, the Grotesque Dancer; and at the foot of the paper was an extract from the *Sheffield Sporting News*:

Gaiety Palace: The feature of the evening is the engagement of Young Tichborne, or, as he styles himself, 'The Claimant's Bootlace.' He has six fingers and one thumb on each hand, plays the Picco, sings and dances well, and is in fact a novelty.

We even find Young Tichborne advertised at the Six Crowns in Woolwich as singing 'Six Fingers and a Thumb'. That he should not only acquiesce but actively co-operate in marketing this exaggeration of his own disability—about which he felt so much self-humiliation in private—was no doubt due to desperate economic pressures. If he was to be noticed among the crowd scrambling for dates, he needed a special attraction. Talent, he was taught, was not enough; or he did not have quite enough talent, he was told, to pull in the business; and so he made game of his own affliction in order to survive in that little theatrical jungle. And later, one supposes, in revulsion against this phase in his *éducation sentimentale*, he blamed it all on the agent.

For all the hardships and humiliations that Harry Relph may have endured on his zigzag travels around England in blackface between the ages of twelve and seventeen, he was a fortunate, even prosperous boy, compared with hundreds of thousands of his working-class—even lower-middle-class—contemporaries. When he was 'showing', he earned £2 a week and upwards: at the same period Charles Coborn, working as a City clerk, was paid only fifteen shillings—and Coborn was fifteen years Harry's senior. And all the time Harry was advancing his self-education: he learned to play the piano (in spite of his fingers), the one-string fiddle and the cello—this became his favourite instrument, and cello solos featured in his early act. He learned to read and write music, and to make his own musical arrangements, playing on at least one occasion in an orchestra pit. He learned to dance on points, well enough to parody precisely a ballerina; and to dance in outsize clogs, or big boots, as they became known—which he was later to elaborate into a speciality that made his name, though he did not invent the genre or the name. Big boots seem to have originated from the union of the native clogs with the outsize flat shoes (flip-flops) used for additional comic effect by 'nigger' comedians. Clog

28

dancing was all the rage for some years: it set Dan Leno on the road to fame, after he had won a belt in 1883 as 'Champion Clog Dancer of the World'—in Oldham! There was a time when, as the manager George Adney Payne recalled, 'audiences would have nothing but what the profession knew as "clog wallopers".' Apart from perfecting his clog walloping, Harry also picked up a smattering of French and other languages (he proved to be a natural linguist) from the Continental performers on the road—jugglers, conjurors, dancers and acrobats. He studied their techniques and their training, using acrobatic exercises to strengthen his muscles and enhance his dancing effects. He even appeared briefly in a triple bar act. He studied, too, the ways and means, the do's and don'ts, of comedians, and the curious variations in the temperature and temperament of audiences. He sketched and painted, whenever he could afford the time, and he read a great deal trying to make up for the missing education he felt was his due. And while he gained knowledge he lost weight: 'I got thin when I began to work hard.' The dancing did it. Young Tichborne was no longer fat: merely small. Persistently so.

One of the few self-portraits of that time emerges in a story he told his family about an emergency when he arrived at a railway station to find that he didn't have enough money in his pocket for the fare home and didn't know how to get it. He remembered that as he sat outside the station, writing to his mother in Gravesend, he could not stop crying; and the tears not only smudged his careful copper plate but fell into the bag of sweets he was clutching for consolation, making them stickier than they ought to have been, and getting the stickiness on to the letters, which made him cry all the more. That backward glance at the little lost showman—half-ironic, half self-pitying—is almost the only glimpse of his private feelings in that period that he gave to his last wife. Harry seems to have closed his mind firmly to those early experiences; and it is not unduly sentimental, we suggest, to deduce that they left lacerations he preferred to forget, more painful than those caused by being short of the price of a ticket home. (His father died in 1881 at the age of ninety-one when Harry was fourteen: he was buried in Fawkham with his father, mother and first wife.)

There was little time for *play* in Harry Relph's life as a boy and an adolescent: he missed out on a world of childhood and the teens that more protected, cosseted middle-class children took for granted. Yet all the while he was learning something beyond the

29

common ken: how to be a great performer, like no other artist on the boards; how to make not only a virtue but a triumph out of being different from everybody else.

The fact that at sixteen Harry looked like a boy of twelve (and still did so when he was nearly twenty) was in one way a business asset. Children were very popular on the Victorian stage: dwarfs and midgets even more so in the halls, fairs and free-and-easies. London attractions in the early 1880's included Mr Charles Pearson, the Sussex Dwarf; Colonel D. Ulpts, the Tyrolese Midget; General Tiny Mite; and such performers as Tiny Tim, Little Pedro and Little Sandy. Harry Relph was certainly not a midget, nor was he a dwarf, although he has often been inaccurately described as one. He had none of the characteristics of many dwarfs, like an outsize head, a humped back or a clumsy gait. He was a dapper, graceful man. But, as he discovered by the time he was seventeen, he was abnormally small. He had, in effect, stopped growing around the age of ten, when he left school, and he never grew taller than four feet six inches. Already he was painfully conscious that he was set apart from other boys, because of the deformity of his hands. Now he at last brought himself to realize, when he could no longer ignore the painful truth, that he was—as he saw it—a freak in a much more manifest way. Nearly all the performers he admired, the people he liked, the girls he fell for were—and were bound to be—at least half a foot taller. The discovery must have at first appeared as a major catastrophe, destroying his plans for the future, as he fought his way through the rowdy, coarse and often cruelly competitive world of the 'spittoons'.

Yet Harry set out, with courage and skill, to make the best of it; not in a spirit of resignation, but in a positive and creative way, by seeking to turn his liabilities into assets. He did so in minor as well as major matters: for instance, he travelled between dates at half-price on a child's ticket whenever he felt he could get away with it. When at the age of seventeen he handed his ticket in one day at Kidderminster, he had clearly been chancing his luck too long. The ticket collector said, 'Look here, young fellow, how old are you?'

'Fourteen', said Harry.

'And how long have you been fourteen?'

'Oh, about three years or so.'

The collector hauled him before the station-master; they decided to let Harry go after a long interrogation and solemn warning; but he never travelled at half-price again, so he said.

If he was to remain unusually small, Harry decided, then he would make his size help to make him unusually famous. If people of 'normal' height found him funny to look at, so much the better for his act. As he said, in his later heyday:

> I never complained about my size: in fact, I arrived at the conclusion, when I first entered my teens, that a diminutive stature might be an aid to humour, and it has been an important part of my stock-in-trade ever since.

His jokes and his patter rubbed in the fact of his size; his costume emphasized it; his anecdotes about himself harped on it—(although off the stage he was quick to resent anyone who seemed to be staring at him or patronizing him because of his height). It was appropriate that, having accepted his destiny—to be almost a dwarf in stature—he should take a new professional name that vaunted it as a trademark.

Until the winter of 1884 Harry Relph had been billed as Young Tichborne, the Pocket Mackney; or Young Tichborne, Little Black Storm; or Young Tichborne, the Picco Soloist; or—a sign of the times, earlier that year—Tiny Tich. But in November 1884 he changed his professional name, for good, to Little Tich—or Little Titch, as it was first spelled in the advertisements. He 'reduced' his name, he said, because 'The Claimant was out, he went round the halls lecturing and the names got mixed up.' Arthur Orton had been released in October, and was touring the country in an attempt to reopen the case. The change of name, however, also coincided with Harry Relph's acquisition of an agent, one of the brightest and youngest in the business, who secured for Harry his first engagement at a London music hall. An advertisement in the *Era* on 25 October 1884 marked this turning-point in Harry's career. It read:

> Little Titch (Negro Comedian) begs to announce that he has placed his Business Arrangements in the hands of Mr Edward Colley, and will make his first Appearance in London on Monday, November 3, at the Foresters and Marylebone.

'Little Titch'—'acknowledged to be one of the most Eccentric Negro Comedians Extant'—was then playing at the hall where he had made his professional debut; and it was here at Barnard's in

31

Chatham that he was introduced in October to Edward Colley, a top agent at twenty-five, who henceforward took him in hand, till Colley's premature death five years later.

The evolution of music hall in Victorian times has frequently been defined as 'from pot-house to palace'. When Harry Relph arrived in London in 1884, metropolitan music halls were roughly halfway in that rapid progress. There were no fewer than 347 halls: eighty per cent of them were public house concert rooms, 'harmonic meeting places', and other places of public assembly without real stages, proscenium arches or orchestra pits, but among the main showplaces were the first London Pavilion, the second Alhambra and the third Oxford. Chairmen were still in power, but they had little more than a decade left to them. Artists' salaries were beginning to soar. Programmes included up to thirty items, all tightly timed. A performer in demand could play three, four or five halls in a night by careful management, jumping into a waiting hansom and driving from stage door to stage door. Cooler spirits, with fewer dates, might even manage to do this by omnibus.

Harry Relph's double debut in the metropolis was split between two small, old-established halls, still close to the pubs from which they developed: the Marylebone in Marylebone High Street, a first-floor 200-seater (born nearly thirty years earlier from the ground-floor Rose of Normandy); and the Foresters in Cambridge Road, Mile End Road (an offspring of the Artichoke pub, and the place where Dan Leno made his London debut the following year). Harry was due to appear at the Marylebone at 9.5, and Foresters at 10.15. On his first appearance, he said:

> I did not know how quickly the programme had to be worked to get it all in. I had two songs, and after the first I rushed upstairs to my dressing room, changed and rushed down again, shouting, 'Ring up! Ready!' But I only got looks of blank astonishment. Another turn was on meanwhile, and I was 'off' for the evening.

Billed at Foresters as 'Little Titch, the Funny Little Nigger', at the Marylebone he was 'The Most Curious Comique in Creation.' By the end of November he seemed to have made a hit. Little Tich was appearing in four halls: the Middlesex (at 8 p.m.) the Marylebone (9 p.m.) the Star in Bermondsey (10 p.m.) and

32

Crowders in the Mile End Road (11 p.m.) It was at the Marylebone that he made, initially, the greatest impact: he stayed there for ten consecutive weeks, and won a glowing notice—the first detailed one we can trace—in the *Era* (though it began by acclaiming him as Young Tichborne, not Little Tich):

> We have never of late seen a Nigger impersonator with such an original vein of drollery. It may perhaps be said that the peculiar conformation of Little Tich's legs has something to do with the comicality of his dancing, and that also makes his American song and dance act the funniest thing of the kind that has been seen on the music-hall stage for years; yet in the expression of his face there is a world of humour; while his absurd business in a big boot dance made even that noisy form of amusement attractive. We shall probably hear a great deal more of Little Tich, as he seems to be one of the few that can invest the business of the Negro comedian with any humour.

Marylebone did not see a great deal more, in fact, of Little Tich: only a couple of weeks that summer. But he found work at other second-rank, old-style halls such as the Middlesex in Drury Lane and the Pavilion in the Mile End Road. Both were boisterous places, which served as often painful training-grounds for performers: 'a kind of intermediate school'. Both had distinctive audiences of their own. The Middlesex—better known as the Old Mo' (short for Mogul)—retained the chairman long after he had vanished from other establishments, and his table was a favourite resort of young doctors and medical students on the town from King's College Hospital. A correspondent in the *Era* recalled in 1910 that 'the audience was always on the best of terms with the stars, and conversations were carried on between them over the footlights and between the verses . . . Waiters looking like noblemen in disguise (the only people in evening dress) dispensed stout to the aristocracy in the stalls, while outside the gallery doors coster girls (the professional descendants of Nell Gwynne) sold oranges to wet the whistle of the Mogul "gods".' The Whitechapel Pavilion (not to be confused with the London Pavilion) had a 'rough and cosmopolitan' audience combining the British and foreign sailors and dockers—like those whom Tich knew well from Gravesend—with 'costers in their pearly suits, mingling with the local tradesmen and their families, who came well provided with bags of provisions which they munched

33

happily during the show'. Prostitutes and their pimps were not quite so much in evidence as at the Middlesex.

The experience that halls like these provided was all grist to Little Tich's mill; and the mill was kept in fairly full employment during the two years after his London debut. He also achieved the customary initiation into provincial pantomime, though he had to go a long way to get a minor part. It was at the Royal Princess's in Glasgow, in *Robinson Crusoe,* in 1885/6. As a specialist in blackface he appeared in the small role of a black attendant of King Tum-tum, named Chillingowadaborie after a popular number in the repertoire of Arthur Lloyd, a music-hall Lion Comique of the day. The kindly *Era* gave him another glowing notice : 'a more genuinely funny performance we have never seen . . . his quiet humour fairly convulsed the audience'.

Yet it seems that in spite of a good start Little Tich failed to establish himself with London audiences, once the initial novelty of his act had worn off. He often played no more than one hall in a night, and he did not penetrate to the key dates such as the Oxford and the London Pavilion. 'The Most Curious Comique in Creation' had to fall back from time to time on the provincial small halls. And at the Middlesex and Pavilion his name appeared in small letters on the bills, not far from the 'wines and spirits'. As he said in later years, 'I didn't seem to catch on at all.' For all his talent, and his agent's efforts, Harry Relph had to go to America before he was really 'discovered' by British managers.

4

FROM NEW YORK TO DRURY LANE

The music hall audience is terribly trying to the artiste. One night they are all applause, and the next night, for no apparent reason you find them perfectly cold and sometimes spiteful. I could not get a hand at first for the song, 'I could do with a bit'. I threw it aside, and a year later when I tried it again it was a tremendous success. How do you account for that?

Little Tich

Little Tich is a Negro comedian of decided ability and considerable humour. Though he has but small vocal powers, he makes the utmost use of them, and the music of his songs is always well written and taking in style. This gentleman's comic business is as original as it is genuinely comic and his doings create the heartiest and healthiest laughter . . . his step dancing and also his clog dancing are alike excellent.

That was how Harry Relph appeared to a friendly reviewer from the *Era* in the summer of 1886, when he was nearly nineteen; and that is how he must have seemed to the American impresario Tony Pastor, who saw Harry in action at Gatti's-in-the-Road, the little music hall in the Westminster Bridge Road (*not* the Gatti's in Villiers Street, known as Gatti's-in-the-Arches). Pastor, who came to Europe every year on a talent-spotting expedition, signed him up for his Gaiety Company, to tour the States for three months in 1887. This company, like its London namesake, specialized in spectacular burlesque; and Harry was to play a small part in a burlesque version of 'The Hunchback of Notre Dame' at £10 a week. For America this was small pay; but in England at this phase in his career he could earn such an amount only by playing four halls a night in London, a situation that he had enjoyed for no more than two weeks at his advent and did not then seem likely to be repeated. (By that winter, Marie Lloyd was earning £100 a week—after only a year at work.) What is more, the money was guaranteed; he would have the privileged

35

opportunity of seeing the United States, and gaining new experience; and—a decisive factor—he liked Tony Pastor, more than any British managers with whom he had so far dealt. 'Mr Pastor is one of the kindest men I know', said Harry later. 'He treats you right off as a friend.'

Tony Pastor, then nearly fifty, was a shrewd, avuncular, showman of Falstaffian girth, a pious Catholic with a personal portable backstage shrine. He had started in show business at about seven as a child prodigy, with Barnum; at ten he was doing a blackface song-and-dance act in a touring circus; at fourteen he was a ringmaster; and he became a leading singer of topical songs before, at twenty-four, he opened his first theatre in New York. Later he turned a Bowery hall into Pastor's Opera House, and launched a touring variety company. Five years before he saw Little Tich, Pastor opened the first really 'clean' variety show in America at his Fourteenth Street Theatre. It was, as the historian of American vaudeville, Douglas Gilbert, says, 'a canny bid to double the audience by attracting respectable women' : hitherto only 'gals on the trampish side' had attended such entertainments. But the mission of the 'double audience' was energized not only by Pastor's commercialism but by his Puritanism. In signing up Little Tich he showed his recognition of the man's blazing talent, but he was influenced by the fact that Relph's comedy was unusually free from sexual or scatological innuendo, and provoked 'the *healthiest* laughter', to repeat our opening quotation. Like Tony Pastor, Little Tich believed in clean entertainment.

After playing that Christmas in an East End *Cinderella* (as King Mischief, at the Whitechapel Pavilion), Harry Relph set off early in 1887 for his discovery of America with his cello, his picco and his big boots. ('I went under the protection of my cello.') He scored such a success in *Esmeralda*, partly because of the Big Boot dance, that Pastor engaged him for two further seasons, so that he was on the road throughout the States for some nine months. That November, at the end of his engagement, he was presented by Pastor at a celebratory party in New York with a gold medal (inscribed 'a mark of appreciation') and, later, with a big white Bohemian dog, Cheri, who was to become an institution of the Relph household in London. Such presentations were not uncommon in the theatrical world, and Little Tich was to receive many more tributes through the years; but he never forgot these gifts from his first American manager and the opportunities he had been given in the States. Tony Pastor was, he often said in later life, his 'greatest benefactor'—even if he didn't *pay* enough.

Harry's work with the Pastor company had attracted the attention of the Chicago State Opera Company, which put him under a two-year contract at a bigger salary than he had ever earned before, said to be 150 dollars a week. But first he returned to England to fulfil a pantomime engagement at the Theatre Royal, Brighton. Billed as 'Tiny Titch' (a sign that he had still not established himself at home), he played the Emperor Muley in *Dick Whittington* until mid-February. In June he opened in Chicago in *The Crystal Slipper,* a Cinderella burlesque written by the Gaiety author-designer Alfred Thompson (with Harry B. Smith), and he justified his salary by scoring a personal success—apparently in the Buttons role—so notably that the show ran for over ten months. Harry played for sixteen weeks in Chicago, seven in Boston, five in New York, and also appeared in Philadelphia, Minneapolis, Williamsburg, Baltimore, Buffalo, St Louis, Cincinatti, Kansas City, Milwaukee, Detroit, Cleveland, Pittsburg and Washington, more or less in that order. Hailed in Chicago as 'undoubtedly one of the most successful comedians the stage has seen for many decades' and in Pittsburg as 'the most notable speciality performer that has been seen in this country for years'. Little Tich received notices like this from the American press :

> His diminutive body seems strung on wires, and he dances and cavorts around with a grace and nimbleness which many of the ballet girls try in vain to imitate. Then he sings catchy songs in a quaint voice, exploits in shoes almost as big as himself, plays excruciatingly on the Chinese fiddle, is a good performer on the violincello, and awakes the echoes with a whistle called a picco . . . His 'business' changes nightly in some feature. Sometimes it is a new step, at others it is a grimace of extraordinary grotesqueness, and again a Terpsichorean exertion which arouses the enthusiasm of the audience . . . His dancing is entirely original.

The Crystal Slipper not only gave Harry Relph, at the age of twenty, new prosperity and prestige : it brought two important changes in his life. He met an English dancer in the company, Laurie Brooks, whom he married in Cook County, Illinois in 1889.

37

(The story of that marriage, as far as we know it, is told in a later chapter.) The second change was that he stopped blacking up, an action which, as one American critic said, 'doubled his comic ability'. He later explained that at rehearsals the American producer said to him, on seeing his negro make-up, 'Boy, you won't need that here. This is where they come from. We raise 'em here. A deaf mute with one eye could see you ain't a coon. None of the folks here will think you're funny.' In fact, 'the folks' went on demanding nigger minstrel make-up from many of their own entertainers: according to Douglas Gilbert, 'the majority of comedy acts in vaudeville were blackface in the eighties'. It was a blackface comic with a British accent, no doubt, that they resisted. Harry was very nervous about showing his own face. 'So very strange did I feel without my burnt cork that I quite expected the audience to throw bricks at me. On the contrary, they approved. I determined, then and there, to bid goodbye to the old style of make-up—for ever.' And he never put on burnt cork again—except, reluctantly, in one British pantomime.

It was during his American years, moreover, that he perfected the presentation of the Big Boot dance. At first his boots—'long clogs', as they were once called—had been only ten inches in length; then twelve inches; then fourteen. By the time Harry was playing in 'Blue Beard' they were twenty-eight inches; which was precisely the right length, he had discovered, for his height in achieving the special effects by which he partly made his name. Harry used to explain their length by saying it was an accident: that, having discovered a new pair of 'big boots' was shorter than he had ordered, he told the shoemaker in a fury to make them size $2\frac{1}{2}$; they were, in fact, made $2\frac{1}{2}$ *feet*; but he somehow managed to use the result. The truth appears to be simpler and duller: that in carefully elaborating and perfecting his act Harry changed his boots until he had found exactly the right length.

On his American tour he would quick-change into his big boots in the wings between numbers. But one day as he rushed off the stage to make his change an officious stage manager snapped at him, 'It's taking you far too long to change here. You'll have to put the boots on in front of the audience.' And he threw them on to the stage. The disconcerted and furious comedian ran back, picked them up, signed to the leader of the band and, while they played 'till ready' music, he struggled into the boots in full view of the public, carrying it off as best he could as if this were part of his act. And from then on it was, because the 'putting on business', as he called it thereafter, was an instant hit. He elaborated and modulated this business, like all his stage work, through the years, sometimes making his entrance with the boots tucked underneath his arm, sauntering casually on; sometimes having them thrown to him. But however varied the entrance might be, from that moment in America he always donned his boots in front of the audience, with deliberate difficulty. As he said in later years, 'I am able to make so much play of putting them on now that I hardly need to dance in them.'

In spite of his success in *The Crystal Slipper,* and the promise of another Chicago engagement, Harry Relph came back to London after *The Crystal Slipper* closed in April 1889—officially for 'a few weeks rest before returning for another twelve months tour' (as the advertisement announced), but apparently nursing the thought that if he made a hit now he might stay at home. His new wife, perhaps, was eager to get back to London. Or perhaps it was Harry who was homesick. He took—most unusually—a large advertisement in the *Era* on 4 May, announcing that he had 'Just Returned from America' with 'an entirely new Repertoire of Specialities, originated by himself and performed in his own quaint fashion. The Seasick Sailor, The Voodoo Venus, The Professor and the Violincello, and The Inimitable and Wonderful Big Boot Dance.' With Edward Colley's help he was engaged at the Empire in Leicester Square ('The Most Beautiful and Luxurious Theatre in Europe', its advertisements claimed) which had opened only eighteen months before as a new-style, unprecedentedly comfortable showplace, with thick carpets and seats like armchairs. He was paid £12 a week, his best yet in London. Dan Leno, Marie Lloyd, Chirgwin the White-Eyed Kaffir, and 'Sir' Sam Redfern were on the bill. They were also appearing at the Paragon and Canterbury, but Little Tich was not. That was one bad augury. Another was that he was advertised as 'Little Titch'. Moreover he was put on as second turn, a bad position. Business at the Empire was poor. He was not well received. And the manager, giving him two weeks notice, wrote to Colley that Little Tich was not worth *half* his salary. The manager was Augustus Harris, whom Harry was to meet shortly under different circumstances.

Harry was bitterly hurt and disappointed by his Empire experiences, believing that he hadn't been given a fair chance. 'After six weeks in England I returned [in June] to America disgusted with fortune.' His disgust could scarcely have persisted; for in the next Chicago State Opera production, *Bluebeard Junior,* he scored another personal hit. Although the show was not as successful as its predecessor, it toured for several months. Harry left it before the end of the tour, however, and long before his contract expired. He liked America very much: indeed, he told pressmen that he thought seriously of settling in the States, but the climate didn't suit him. He never forgot, in later years, how much of his fame and fortune he owed initially to American audiences. But he liked England better. And he longed to take the measure, once again, of the London music halls. What's more, his wife was pregnant; and they wanted the child to be born at home in Britain.

When Harry returned in the autumn of 1889 (his son, Paul, was delivered two months later) he found that his American success had turned the tide of his fortune. He was, he insisted, just the same artist as he was in 1886. He had given up burnt cork; any other difference could only be in the eyes of managers and customers. But *they* insisted that he *had* changed. To his fury, reviewers said things like 'he is a much improved comedian since his visit to America' or 'he seems to have absorbed some of the Yankee spirit of mirth into his composition, and is droller than ever now'. They may well have been right: success often breeds success, and his American accolades must have given a huge injection of confidence to the ever-vulnerable and self-critical Harry. He may not have changed *what* he did; but *how* he did it, and *how* he saw himself, was inevitably influenced by his transatlantic experiences, and he underestimated the liberating effect on his facial mime of giving up 'working black'. In any event London critics said increasingly that he was indescribably and uniquely funny, and more important, London audiences agreed with them. Under Edward Colley's guidance he found himself, for a time, playing three or four halls a night again.

Most significantly, Little Tich penetrated at last to the heart of the West End—to the London Pavilion in Piccadilly Circus. The Pav, as it was affectionately known, was built on the site of a stable yard belonging to a coaching inn in Tichborne Street, a name that dated from long before the Claimant's time. When it opened as a music hall in 1861 it was publicized as 'the first

40

music hall de luxe' in the West End; but its luxuries were demolished in 1884 when the Circus was enlarged and Shaftesbury Avenue was broached. The new Pavilion—of which the façade survives today—was opened in 1885, still with a chairman and marble-topped tables. But within a year the Syndicate Halls Company took it over and changed all that. Out went the chairman and the tables. In came the first tip-up seats, and—what is more—you could *reserve* them. But there was still a pipeline to the old tradition: the backs of these revolutionary seats had ledges on which you could safely put down your glass between swigs or sips. And although in 1889 the Pav was no longer the most comfortable and ultra-modern of variety theatres—the Empire had eclipsed it in that respect—it could claim to be *the* West End music hall, combining as it did something of the atmosphere of the old regime and the comforts of the new. The Oxford was the same age and enjoyed a similar prestige, but it was less *central;* and that, increasingly, mattered.

Within six months of his return to England Little Tich had reached the top of his profession. Yet the main credit was due, so he felt at the time, not to London, but to America—and Manchester. Thomas W. Charles, manager of the Princes Theatre there, saw Harry at the Pav, was deeply impressed, and engaged him for the 1889/90 pantomime, *Babes in the Wood.* He played Bantam, a page to the bad Baron. It was a small part, but Harry made it a big one, and it remained one of his favourites. Praising him as 'very clever', the *Manchester Guardian* critic wrote:

He goes through several wild and wonderful step-dances, knocking himself down and flinging his legs about with an awkward gravity that makes his movements extremely laughable. His dance in long flat wooden shoes is a triumph of eccentric step-dancing—accurate, elaborate with many different gymnastic contortions, and full of whimsical and extravagant antics. It is certainly the most striking thing in the pantomime, and was loudly encored.

On the first night Tich got 'the heartiest applause of the evening' at the final walk-down. The performance became a talking-point in Manchester, and word of it reached London; indeed the Princes pantomimes were known to be among the best in Britain. According to Harry Randall 'there was nothing in London—outside Drury Lane—to compare with them'. Agents and managers

41

came north to see Little Tich, as if he were a new discovery. One visitor was the most influential of all British managers, Augustus Harris: the man who had sacked Harry from the Empire in the previous summer. Harris apparently remembered nothing of the incident (a case, perhaps, of strategic amnesia) and Harry diplomatically decided to forget it, too. For 'Druriolanus', as Harris was dubbed, signed him up on the spot to play in the capital of pantomime, Drury Lane: not just for *one* show but two, and at £36, three times the salary he was getting in Manchester. Tich was not free for the 1890 panto at the Lane: he had contracted to work for Tom Charles again, as Toddlekins in *Little Bo Peep,* a role (in some senses) made to measure. To quote the *Era*:

> This wonderful little comedian figures first as a two-year-old babe, with his feeding bottle, and in the course of the story he matures to manhood. The idea is a most amusing one, and offers him opportunities of appearing as a baby who can vault into his cradle, as the 'dirty boy' who requires washing, as the precocious youth in a Lord Fauntleroy velvet suit and ruffles . . . and of displaying 'the education of the feet', with the most droll and mirth-provoking humour.

The *Manchester Guardian,* extolling the 'amazing fertility and drollery' with which Tich developed the notion of Toddlekins's evolution, went much further in its praise:

> With a head as bald as polished ivory, with his diminutive proportions, his infantile costume and a peculiarly bland smile rivalling that of the Heathen Chinee, Little Tich is surely the oddest and one of the most diverting figures seen upon the stage. He is a droll in the best sense of the word, and had he lived half a century ago he would have left a mark in English dramatic history as one of our leading English clowns . . . let it not be said that true pantomime is dead or that the art of mimicry is lost while it is possible to enjoy the whimsicalities of such a mime as Little Tich . . . Such a performance is inimitable . . . All Lancashire will feel bound to see it.

Later, at Drury Lane, Tich played much the same role; but with far less enjoyment than in Manchester. *Little Bo Peep* was, he said, the best pantomime he had ever played in. It also broke all Manchester records in box office business and length of run, and the *Era* described it as 'the first of the modern prose-pantomimes'.

Its London revival was projected in 1896, but by then Little Tich was not available.

'I am sure my engagement with Mr Charles was the making of me,' he said in 1891. 'I put it all down to Manchester'; and he continued, till the end of his life, to rank the manager of the Princes among his main benefactors, as a man who—like Tony Pastor—could see more clearly to the heart of talent than the London wheelers and dealers. Tom Charles, who died a few years later (11/11/1895) at fifty-two after being thrown from a pony trap, had made his name as a manager at Nottingham and Glasgow. He was praised by a rival Manchester manager (J. Pitt Hardacre) as 'undoubtedly the first of his time as a producer of pantomime'.

During 1890, between his two Manchester pantomimes, Little Tich established himself in the London music hall, over five years after his debut in the capital, as a bright, particular star of the London Pavilion. A sure sign of his new fame was his appearance for the first time in the cartoons of the trade press—on the cover of *Music Hall* in April, and the following month, more illustriously, in *Entr'acte,* where he was shown (still mis-spelled) in his tutu from his ballet-girl burlesque, with such celebrities as Chirgwin, Harry Randall and Sam Redfern behind him. The occasion was the opening of the Tivoli in the Strand. Its manager had booked Tich, with others, as an inaugural attraction—only to find that the Oxford, the Pavilion and the Canterbury refused to allow their artists to perform at the new showplace. The *Entr'acte* cartoon shows the Pavilion manager saying paternally to Tich and his colleagues, 'Now, you are all very good boys, and we like you very much, but you mustn't go to the Tivoli.' In the end they did; but only after the intrepid opening management had sold out to the Pavilion proprietors.

In his new fame Little Tich became known not only in Manchester and London, but all around the country—often in towns and cities where, some seven to ten years earlier, he had worked in relative obscurity as Young Tichborne. From the start of his celebrity in the music hall until his last curtain he was always more than a London star; but at this decisive phase in his career he did not depend only upon the music halls to achieve his national reputation.

Although Little Tich was essentially a soloist, like all the great music hall performers, show business economics sometimes either obliged him or tempted him to work not only in pantomimes (the seasonal stand-by for most variety artists in the past century) but also in burlesque, musical comedy and revue. The first of these shows, after Tich had made his name in Manchester panto, was *Miss Esmeralda,* a burlesque version of *The Hunchback of Notre Dame* : not, it would seem, the Tony Pastor production in which Harry had toured the USA, but a revised and enlarged version of a Gaiety show staged later in 1887. After seeing Little Tich as Bantam in *Babes in the Wood* the actor-manager Rollo Balmain cast him as Quasimodo, cashing in on his disabilities as well as his specialities (including his burlesque of a ballet girl, inserted in the third act). Tich also scored as a monkey, dancing to a barrel organ, and sang his two earliest song-successes, 'Smiles' and 'I could do, could do, could do with a bit'. This latter song— often invoked affectionately in later memories of Tich—was not, as the title suggests, a prolonged double entendre in the style of Marie Lloyd, but a song about eating, drinking and money. It was written and composed by Walter Tilbury. On the page the words —like those of most comic hits of yesteryear—exude a mortuary chill; but they cannot, for that reason, be excluded from Little Tich's story. Imagination must try to resurrect the comic force of the waif-like imp who sang them.

Whilst looking thro' a window at some puddings smoking hot
It struck me rather forcibly an appetite I'd got;
A nice thick slice on paper, oh how it would go down,
But all my longing was in vain, I hadn't got a 'brown'.

CHORUS : I could do, could do, could do, could do, could do
      with a bit
    I could do, could do, could do, could do, could do
      with a bit
    That pudding looked so nice that I thought once or
      twice
    I could do with a little very well,
    I could do, could do, could do, could do, could do
      with a bit
    I could do, could do, could, could do, could do with
      a bit
    That pudding looked so nice that I thought once
      or twice
    I could do with a little very well.

Now sometimes men go racing and often back a horse
To win them lots of money (which it sometimes does, of course)
And when they go to draw their oof they laugh and smile with
   glee
As I stand by, quite stony-broke, the thought occurs to me

CHORUS: I could do, could do, could do, could do, could do
           with a bit
         I hadn't got my fare, so I thought as I stood there
         I could do with a little very well
         I could do, could do, could do, could do, could do
           with a bit
         I could do, could do, could, could do, could do with
           a bit
         I hadn't got my fare, so I thought as I stood there
         I could do with a little very well

I've got a squalling baby, it howls all day and night
And where that kid gets so much breath from is a mystery quite
If there's a chance to stop it, I should like to know the way
For since its birth I've had no sleep—believe me when I say—

CHORUS: I could do, could do, could do, could do, could do
           with a bit
         The squalling of the child has driven me nearly wild
         I could do with a little very well
         I could do, could do, could do, could do, could do
           with a bit
         I could do, could do, could, could do, could do with
           a bit
         The squalling of the child has driven me nearly wild
         I could do with a little very well

It's awkward when you get so boozed that both your legs give way
You sit down quietly in the street, then hear a policeman say
'Now, you get up and get off home, you beastly drunken whelp
And just look sharp about it too or I'll give you some help'

Spoken: Which is a very fine suggestion under the circum-
         stances and you naturally reply:

CHORUS: I could do, could do, could do, could do, could do
           with a bit
         I could do, could do, could do, could do, could do
           with a bit

I sat there in the cold and the constable I told
I could do with a little very well
I could do, could do, could do, could do, could do
   with a bit
I could do, could do, could, could do, could do with
   a bit
I sat there in the cold and the constable I told
I could do with a little very well.

During 1891, between his second Manchester and his first
Drury Lane pantomime, Little Tich toured Britain as Quasimodo.
He was not seen anywhere nearer the West End than the Elephant
and Castle. Two things caught the attention of most Press observers. One was his inescapable weirdness: 'the oddest of the
odd', he seemed in Bath, and in Birmingham he appeared like 'a
being sprung out of one of Grimm's fairy tales'. A Brighton
observer described him, more temperately, as 'overpoweringly
quaint, and small, and novel'. His 'very littleness' seemed so
exceptional that a Portsmouth critic described him as 'some three
feet in height' (an under-estimate of eighteen inches). Tich's
other most obvious attraction was his dancing. This was acclaimed
as 'a marvel of skill and comicality' (in Leicester) and 'an ideal
exhibition of terpsichorean art' (in Newcastle). 'There are certain
of his steps and twists in dancing which are done quicker than the
eye can follow them,' said the *Birmingham Post*, 'and which remind one of nothing so much as the map of an instantaneous
camera disk, or a clever card-pass.' His legs, as a later critic put
it, could 'wink'. According to the *Sussex Daily News*:

> No one can have any idea of the variety of steps until he has
> seen Little Tich's galvanic legs. One of his songs says he is
> 'highly educated in the feet'. But that underestimates his
> powers. Highly educated! He is far away the most marvellous
> dancer the stage knows. But any description of his movements
> is impossible.

He was, it appeared in Northampton, 'seemingly not troubled
with bones'. The Isle of Man found him 'an undoubted genius',
and in Blackpool he seemed 'the funniest little mortal we ever
saw on the stage; and old theatre lovers say the same of him'. This
kind of tribute was to be repeated throughout Little Tich's touring career. So was the occasional patronizing—even contemptuous

46

Boy in blackface: touring the provinces in the 1880s as a Negro Impersonator

In the 'big boots', at 23, after his British 'discovery'

The Pirate, 1905

The General, 19[

The Gendarme, 1918

LITTLE TICH GOES GAY

One of Little Tich's most
celebrated roles, the Spanish
Senora; left, 1893; top left, 1901;
above, 1924

Characteristic French caricature, from the 'autobiography' 'Little Tich' – ghosted by Sax Rohmer-published in 1911

Early photograph, c.1890

The Tax Collector, 1917

The Huntswoman, 1917

NEW ● STAR
Music Hall and Picture Gallery,
COULSON-ST. (Bottom of Snighill), SHEFFIELD.

Proprietor - - - - - - - Mr A. MILNER.

Programme
For MONDAY, SEPT. 10th, 1883, and during the Week.

NOTICE—The Number on the programme, corresponding with that exhibited on the right hand side of the Orchestra indicates the artiste who is occupying the stage.

PART FIRST.

Overture at Seven o'clock........ .... THE BAND

1— Comic Song .... ALIC DAY

2—Serio-Comic Song............ ....Miss MARIE SANTLEY

3 — Lancashire Song.. .... WILL TOWNLEY

4—Serio-Comic Song .... Miss DAISY VICTOR

5—Comic Song .... WILLL BRAMHALL

6—Negro Song........ ....YOUNG TICHBORNE

7—Song........ ....Miss BEATRICE STANFORD

PART SECOND.

1—Song and Cornet .... ALIC DAY

2—Serio-Comic Song .... Miss MARIE SANTLEY

3—Lancashire Song......... ....WILL TOWNLEY

4—Serio-Comic Song...... ....Miss DAISY VICTOR

5—Comic Song...... .... WILL BRAMHALL

6—Negro Song...... ....YOUNG TICHBORNE

7— Song...... ....Miss BEATRICE STANFORD

No one admitted under 18 Years of Age.
No Pass-out Checks allowed.

WILLIAMS, Printer, 27, Paradise Street. Sheffield.

A unique survival: the 1883 programme for a Sheffield music hall in which Little Tich appeared as Young Tichborne

The Pet of the Ballet, c.1891;
alternatively known as La Premiere
Danseuse (top right), this also
featured the Serpentine Dance of
Little Miss Turpentine

IN OTHER PEOPLE'S SHOES.

A NEW SERIES OF CARTOONS BY TOM BROWNE.

THE RIGHT REV
LITTLETICH
LORD
BISHOP
OF
LONDON.

TOM. B.

Turn-of-the-century caricature
by Tom Browne in a series,
'In Other People's Shoes'

Johnny Green, 1915

Alfred Bryan cartoon from
Entr'acte

H.R.H., TO "VARIETY" HIGH LIGHTS: "YOU HAVE BEEN DOING SUCH WONDERS
LATELY AT THE MUSIC-HALLS, THAT I MUST TRY TO ARRANGE A PER-
FORMANCE AT WINDSOR."

ANOTHER SUGGESTION
FOR MESSRS PEARS.!

HERBERT CAMPBELL
AND
LITTLE TICH

With Herbert Campbell in the 1892/3 Drury Lane pantomime, 'Little Bo Beep' drawn by Alfred Bryan

The Indian Chieftain, 1909

The Zoo Keeper, 1909

—note: 'a droll little fellow, with rather a pleasant voice', said a dismissive critic in Edinburgh.

By the time he arrived at the Theatre Royal, Drury Lane for his first pantomime with Augustus Harris, Little Tich was a big name—one of the biggest in the business, scarcely more than two years after his return from America. To be picked for a leading part in a panto at the Lane was considered in his profession to be a supreme accolade. Harris—whose father and grandfather before him were theatre managers—had been staging pantomime at Drury Lane for eleven years when Little Tich joined the pay roll. He had dropped the traditional melodramatic curtain-raiser, giving up the whole evening to the pantomime; he had cut down the harlequinade, which once dominated the panto, to an appendage; and he had exalted the spectacular display by spending large sums of money—well publicized and suitably exaggerated—on expensive costumes and scenic splendours, notably in grand processions where scores of supers filed across the stage in dazzling raiment as The Gods and Goddesses of Ancient Mythology or The Language of Flowers. 'Druriolanus'—or 'Gus', as he was more generally known backstage—liked *quantity*: when he produced the story of Ali Baba, there were not forty but *four hundred* thieves on the boards of Drury Lane. Although he was not the first manager to introduce music hall stars into the Christmas entertainment (that claim has been made for his father) he established the male droll and the 'serio-comic' woman singer as the Dame and Principal Boy respectively, giving fresh life to the old conventions—and plenty of scope for squadrons of girls to underdress as men in seasonal tights. Many Victorians disapproved of this licensed exposure of feminine anatomy to Young Persons, and the contamination of a Theatre Royal by lower-class people with common songs and vulgar jokes; but the Drury Lane annual became a national institution. 'All England wanted to see it, and all the nurseries of the Empire lived on its memory.' Although Little Tich appeared in no more than three of them, his association with Drury Lane undoubtedly set the seal on his reputation in Britain.

The cast of *Humpty Dumpty,* which opened on Boxing Day 1891 and was staged thereafter for many weeks every 'morning' and evening at 1.30 and 7.30, was led by four stars: Marie Lloyd as Princess Allfair, the Principal Girl; Fanny Leslie as King Dulcimer, the Principal Boy; Herbert Campbell and Dan Leno, as the King and Queen of Hearts. Campbell had worked in Harris's Christmas annuals since 1882, Leno since 1888, but it was in this show that they established a comic partnership that lasted until they died, within a few months of each other, thirteen years later. In *Humpty Dumpty,* however, Little Tich—who, as Humpty and the Yellow Dwarf, introduced both the Big Boots dance and his ballerina spoof—was said by most critics to have equalled their success: many observed, with *Punch,* that he was 'first and foremost, both the least and the greatest'. He repeated this individual success the following Christmas as Hop of my Thumb in *Little Bo Peep,* again with Marie Lloyd (Little Red Riding Hood), Dan Leno (Daddy Thumb) and Herbert Campbell (Goody Thumb). Ada Blanche and Marie Loftus were Principal Boy and Girl. And in 1893, as Man Friday in *Robinson Crusoe* with the same principals except Marie Loftus, Little Tich again scored a special hit, although he did not appear until the sixth scene, and even more time than usual was consumed by Gus's processions—notably, The History of England in Twenty Minutes, which not surprisingly took a bit longer than that to parade and disperse: on the first night, a *hundred* minutes.

Robinson Crusoe was Tich's last pantomime for Augustus Harris, who died suddenly at forty-four, two years after its run ended, and it was also his last pantomime at Drury Lane. Why? It was certainly not because Little Tich had failed to please the public. For many people he had even eclipsed Leno; though it may be said that Dan had not yet touched his peak. Nor was Tich's departure due, it seems, to any backstage siroccos: Marie Lloyd and Leno were, and remained, his friends.

The theatrical historian, Maurice Willson Disher, put it on record that Tich was 'made the scapegoat' in a row over the impropriety of Marie Lloyd singing 'A Saucy Bit of Crackling' in *Robinson Crusoe.* She had, in fact, already sinned against the Harris canon in 'Crusoe's' predecessor when, as Little Red Riding Hood, having chastely retired for the night, she suddenly decided to liven things up before putting out the light by getting out of bed, taking an unscripted look underneath it to see if Little Red Riding Hood had everything she needed, and then—disappointed in her quest—wandering around the stage in search of it, to the accompaniment of shocked but delighted laughter. To say what *it* was, exactly, appeared to be beyond the capacity of most reviewers; and Marie's mischievous wheeze seemed unspeakably vulgar to the Puritan minority who in Britain so often succeed in prescribing what the majority ought to see, read and hear. Augustus Harris gave her a solemn warning to watch it. Perhaps, as W. MacQueen Pope suggested, it was 'that mischievous imp', Little Tich, who sparked off this episode by whispering from the wings 'Look under the bed, Marie.' Yet Tich could hardly be blamed either for Marie's song in *Robinson Crusoe,* or for his own material which, as Willson Disher acknowledged, was 'inoffensive'—never risking the moral damage of indicating the presence, or rather the absence, of a chamber-pot.

More plausibly it is argued that Harris had to cut his losses on *Robinson Crusoe* (said to be £30,000) and economized by cutting out Little Tich and Marie Lloyd from his next pantomime. He decided that he had a surfeit of comedians: it seemed impossible for him to conceive that he might also be suffering from a surfeit of spectacle, so that his galaxy of comic talent was—and continued to be—obscured by pageants and processions.

The fact is that Little Tich had already revealed, even before *Robinson Crusoe* opened, that he would not be returning to Drury Lane. For this there were two reasons, though he indicated only one of these to reporters: that there wasn't enough room for him in a Harris production. As he said in one interview, there was less opportunity of making a hit as a solo performer, 'now that a pantomime is principally spectacular. In the provinces they still stick to the old-fashioned lines, and give the principal characters a chance, but it seems to me that nowadays in London our performances serve only as a peg to hang processions and ballets on.' Or, as he put it more succinctly to another journalist during 'Crusoe' rehearsals, 'A comedian doesn't get much chance there at Drury Lane. He may be stuck up in his dressing room for an hour while they're proceshing on the stage.' What chances there were, moreover, had to be shared among four star comics. For all his personal and professional pride, Harry Tich might have tolerated that overcrowding and lack of opportunity if Augustus Harris had made it worth his while, but Harris didn't. He was already spending too much, he decided, on comedy. Even if Little Tich had not already resolved to quit, Harris could not have come to terms with him after the financial disaster of *Robinson Crusoe*. For a music hall comic to work at Drury Lane offered him, in Harris's view, one of life's glittering prizes, irrespective of

49

salary. As Gus no doubt pointed out to Harry, Leno had started there a few years earlier on a joint salary, for his wife and himself, of £28. (Not until after Harris's death did Leno reach £80 a week at the Lane.) Tich found this argument unconvincing. Once he had finished his third panto he wanted a great deal more money than Harris was prepared to pay, if he were to return to the Lane: £100 a week. As Harry Randall says in his autobiography, 'Many took smaller salaries so as to be able to say they were "from Drury Lane".' Harry Tich could say that, if he chose; he chose a bigger salary. So after the run of *Robinson Crusoe* was over, he left Drury Lane for ever. Next Christmas he was back in Manchester, where he was undisputed ruler of the roost, and spectacle was kept in its place. He never appeared again in a pantomime in London.

For some six years—between 1896 and 1902—he also kept away from London music halls. As he explained in an interview in 1900:

> I don't think it is worth while going back to London to do three or four turns (a night) when I can get as much money in the provinces for doing one turn. Another thing: when you work so many halls you cannot show your versatility the same. You are only allowed, say, ten minutes at each hall; whereas when you are in the provinces you can have half an hour in which to do your turn.

There was another aspect to his unwillingness to work three or four halls a night: by its nature Little Tich's act was far more taxing and demanding than that of a stand-up comic and singer like George Robey or Harry Lauder. For him it wasn't only a matter of delivering jokes and performing songs: he frequently had to give one eccentric dance in addition to the gruelling Big Boot number. By the time he started working regularly in London again, the old practice of working three or more halls in a night had been dropped. But even with one performance nightly he found the physical strain increasingly hard to bear. 'Oh, *how* I envy Robey sometimes,' he said. 'I have to nearly kill myself every night.'

During this period Harry's mother died in Gravesend of a hernia, after trying to move furniture at home. She was only fifty-eight. Harry was away in Europe at the time, and as none of the family told him—perhaps because, unaccustomed as they were to the peripatetic life-style of a variety star, they did not know how to pursue him with telegrams—he did not discover what had happened until some weeks after Mrs Relph had been buried. This upset him deeply, and intensified his sense of alienation from his family (Agnes always excepted). More than ever before, he was a loner: his wife and son meant all the more to him.

5

LORD TOM NODDY

It's the lesser of two evils to be as I am. People don't realise the amount of problems *giants* have.

Little Tich

Throughout Little Tich's career the variety stage—the perilous preserve of extreme individualists like him—remained his element. Yet soon after his rise to the summit he attempted, as other music hall artists had done, to establish a foothold in a different kind of theatre. Keeping in mind the success of *Miss Esmeralda,* the profits that managers could make, and their reluctance to pay him what he considered his due, Harry formed his own company to produce musical plays in 1895, and made a ceremonial farewell to the halls. To bid him goodbye a Grand Benefit Night was staged in November at the Metropolitan (always known as 'the Met') in the Edgware Road, at which some eighty colleagues appeared. They included Ada Blanche, Herbert Campbell, Chirgwin, Tom Costello, Gus Elen, Lillie Langtry, Marie Lloyd, George Robey and Harriet Vernon. After performing two of his own numbers and the Big Boots dance, Tich was presented with a laurel wreath almost as large as himself.

The first tailor-made production (and probably the most successful) was *Lord Tom Noddy,* which reached London the following year in September 1896. Written and produced by George Dance, one of Harry's partners in the company, it ran only two months at the Garrick, though it did better on tour. The story, rather more than usually inane, involved Harry—as the hard-up fortune-hunting aristocrat of the title—in a romantic encounter with his former nurse, who had fallen in love with him in his infancy. Here is the song in which he established his character:

I'd an ancestral home, old and rich,
    A library fit for a sage,
And family portraits, all which
    I sold on my coming of age.
My taste is for fast-trotting gees
    And bow-wows that worry and kill
And dens where you sit at your ease
    And witness a jolly good mill;
And clubs where a supper is served
    With Cliquot, and Moet, and Pom
And rarebits and revels—the King of the Revels
    Is Good Old Tom.

Chorus
    I'm Lord Tom Noddy
    Lord Tom Noddy
As smart as London makes 'em and as warm as whisky and toddy.
    Yes, I'm Lord Tom Noddy,
    Lord Tom Noddy
A fin de siecle nobleman is Good Old Tom.

'Almost all the fun of the play,' according to the *Glasgow Herald*, on the production's second visit to that city, 'rests in physical contrast . . . The audience roared with laughter to see tiny Little Tich nursed in the lap of . . . a stalwart Scotchwoman nearly double his height; and afterwards running between the legs of her gigantic brother' (Picton Roxborough, said to be the tallest actor on the British stage. He was cast with Tich again in the following year's pantomime at Manchester). But, for all that, the Glasgow critic admired Tich's 'extremely grotesque' dancing, and 'the easy grace which always marks his performance . .' The most remarkable thing about this feeble little show (in which Sybil Arundale made her London debut) was the virulence that it provoked in otherwise temperate critics: a savage spleen from which Harry Relph was the main sufferer. One reviewer described him as a 'debauched homunculus', and the show as 'a lamentable desecration of the theatre' and 'a perversion of the functions of the stage'. That eminent critic and Ibsenite, Shaw's friend William Archer, went a good deal further, in the *World*. It was, he said, 'an amazing spectacle to be presented on one of the leading stages of a civilized country. To be quite just, it contains none of the deliberate indecency to which some authors devote the best

53

part of their invention; nor is it, in point of story, much more inept than the general run of its class. But words fail me to describe the sordid, squalid spirit that animates its garish body, or to depict the incoherent world of foolish knaves and knavish fools to which it introduces us.' The prime squalor, for Mr Archer, was what he described as 'the personality of a performer known as "Little Tich", a Quasimodo of the music halls, whose "talent" lies in a grotesque combination of agility with deformity.'

> It seems inhuman to dwell on, or even allude to, his physical misfortune; while to ignore it is in fact to betray the cause—not of art, which has nothing to do with the matter—but of ordinary good feeling and humanity. I have seen 'Little Tich' before, in the distance, so to speak, at Drury Lane. The grotesque surroundings of pantomime seemed his natural habitat; he appeared to enjoy his antics, and one accepted him as a gnome in the fairy world. But to see him at close quarters in a small theatre, figuring as a real human being, and the hero, forsooth, of what purports to be a love-story! . . . He, poor fellow, cannot help his diminutiveness, his crookedness, his superfluity of fingers, and if he can make money by exhibiting these things, who shall blame him for doing so? The true hideousness is that of the society which pays to see and laugh at such spectacles, instead of paying liberally to have them kept out of sight.

Who would have believed that the sensitive and scholarly Archer was capable of such patronizing pomposity, critical myopia and cruelty? Hundreds of less eminent journalists, more intimately acquainted with the music halls on which he turned his back, consistently showed a more delicate sensibility in discussing Little Tich than this embattled Scottish moralist. His review is the only one we have traced throughout Tich's career to comment specifically on Harry Relph's hands. It is saddening that Archer should have allowed his anger with the show, his contempt for 'the cant about art in the music-halls' (as he called it, in the previous year) and his curiously intense revulsion from Little Tich to blind him to the fact that there was, indeed, a major talent wasted in *Lord Tom Noddy*—one of the major talents of the European stage. Yet although Archer's reactions to this particular production were unusually violent, he was not alone either in the instinctive distaste he felt at the sight of Little Tich outside a panto-

54

mime on a 'leading stage', or in the defensive intellectual snobbery that prevented him from seeing anything more in the art of the music-hall than 'the art of elaborate ugliness, blatant vulgarity, alcoholic humour and rancid sentiment. There is far more art . . . in acting of ordinary competence,' he declared, 'than in the cleverest performances the English music hall stage can show.'

It is partly for that reason that we have exhumed this notice, in the context of Little Tich's career: to illustrate that the enthusiasm of writers like Max Beerbohm for the 'golden age' of the variety stage was by no means general. We have also quoted Archer's insults to indicate why, throughout his life, Harry Relph kept on the defensive, armoured against possible repugnance or ridicule; sensitive, retiring and evasive to a degree that seemed, at times, to verge on the pathological. Why was he so *touchy*, some people would ask impatiently. To Harry there seemed a sufficiency of reasons. One of them is reflected in William Archer's review of *Lord Tom Noddy*. 'Few things have been more seriously discussed in theatrical circles,' said the *Era*, with pardonable exaggeration, 'than the curiously offensive personality of the *World* notice of *Lord Tom Noddy* . . . The little man has been deeply distressed.' One nagging legacy of the show for Tich was the appearance on variety bills during the next decade of a couple who billed themselves as 'Lord Tom Doddy (40 inches high) and the Gaiety Belle (nearly 7 feet high)—The Great Novelty Turn.' Here, perhaps, William Archer had a case.

Later, with characteristic self-mockery, Little Tich told several reporters and friends this story about what happened when he went for 'relaxation' to the Alhambra while he was rehearsing for *Lord Tom Noddy*.

A gentleman spoke to me—'Mr Tich, I believe?' I said, 'I don't know, but I will institute inquiries.' He said, 'I hope you are appearing at the Alhambra this evening.'
I said, 'No, I am going to give the halls a rest,' and then swelling with pride, 'I am going to play the star part at the Garrick.'
'Ah well,' said my unknown friend, 'cheer up. It's better than doing nothing.'

Two years later Little Tich tried again to 'give the halls a rest' in a musical comedy called *Billy*, with the score by the composer of *Lord Tom Noddy* (Osmond Carr). Once again he was a

c*   55 member of the sporting aristocracy, as the Hon Billy Vavasour, who, in pursuit of a general's daughter (played by Evie Greene), appeared as a cook, a soldier, a jockey and a page-boy. But although the show enjoyed a fairly successful provincial tour after its opening in Newcastle, it came no nearer the West End than a week in Stoke Newington. After that fiasco Little Tich vowed that he would never appear in a London theatre again: not, at least, in a *play*. But his mind was apparently changed by H. Chance Newton, who claimed in *Idols of the Halls* that he was commissioned 'at a fortnight's notice' to write a piece with con-ductor-composer Georges Jacobi for the opening of the London Hippodrome, an event which, after the traditional delays as-sociated with such openings, occurred in January 1900. *Giddy Ostend,* as they called it, was already in rehearsal when, as Chance Newton put it, 'I began to realize that we were much in need of a first class comedian . . .

> On my pointing this out, and saying that although we had only a week before us, I could write a big part in it to fit a little comedian, behold, Messrs Stoll and Thornton suddenly banged me off to South Shields to engage Little Tich . . . Reading the new part, which I had sketched en route, to the popular Tich at the local hotel, that brilliant and most versatile of variety performers speedily arranged to join us . . .

Whether it happened *quite* like that or not (Little Tich was, in-deed, working South Shields in the first week of December), he scored a notable personal success in *Giddy Ostend,* in spite of the competition from the lake (a leading character in the piece) and its ballet of bathers, not to mention such attractions as Leonidas's cats and dogs and Julius Seeth's twenty-one performing lions. It ran for two months only, (Tich could not, in any case, rearrange other commitments) but it had served its purpose in giving the new showplace a flying—or rather a swimming—start. Together with his appearances in *Lord Tom Noddy* and *Billy,* moreover, this experience was of value to Tich in strengthening his technique and extending his range, fortifying him for the increasing num-ber of character studies that he gave in music halls and, as they were now increasingly called, variety palaces.

Little Tich, however, appeared in no more musical plays until, nearly twenty years after *Giddy Ostend,* he was engaged for the leading part of Jeff (partnered with Mutt) in *The Red Mill* at the Empire in London. Then he played an interpreter, a gendarme, a coster and a detective, and some critical surprise was expressed about the strength and subtlety of his dramatic talents, which were said to be 'wasted' on the variety stage. Yet it was too late, it seemed, for Tich to change direction, even if he had been given more opportunity to do so. He knew where he belonged; and there he stayed until he died, working as a soloist before a music hall audience.

6

INTERNATIONAL STAR

It is before the audience that I seek my effects. I add to them,
eliminate, modify according to reactions in the theatre. I work
like a sculptor who models his statue from what he sees in front
of him. The laughter of the audience serves as my model.

Little Tich

Far more than any of his British contemporaries at the summit
of the variety stage, Little Tich was an international star. In the
quarter-century before the First World War he became a celebrity in many European cities. In Paris, especially, as Max
Beerbohm said, 'he was a *succès fou*—even more than in London.'
And it all began in that decisive year of 1890, after his first
Manchester pantomime. He was invited in the spring to appear
in Vienna at the famous Ronacher's theatre, where he made such
a hit that he was asked back in September for a three month
engagement. When it was over, Tich was presented by the management with a silver cup, and invited back for a further season
in 1891. When that engagement closed, he was given a *gold* cup.
They were the symbols of many rich rewards to be gained in
Europe. Early in 1891 he paid his first visit to Berlin : he is said
to have been the first foreign artist to play two music halls in a
night there. During the next three years he appeared in Hamburg,
Geneva, Lausanne, Rotterdam, Brussels, Nice, Monte Carlo,
Marseilles, Lyons, Seville, Barcelona, and Budapest. St Petersburg
was the one exception in a run of international success; he never
revisited Russia. Inexplicably, he does not seem to have made his
debut in Paris, the scene of his greatest triumphs, until later in
the 1890's. And, strangely enough, he returned only once to the
United States—where he had laid the foundation of his success.
In 1901 he worked for two weeks in New York, where he found
audiences, he said, less receptive than on his first visit—from
which he was still remembered by American critics. There were
many invitations. In 1897, for instance, he was booked to appear
in the following year at Oscar Hammerstein's Olympia; but on

his agent's advice he didn't take up the engagement, and some months later the Olympia closed. Other offers were made for tours, as late as 1926; but from his second engagement at Ronacher's Little Tich's working life was divided between Britain and the Continent, (with two visits to Australia and one to South Africa). For the best part of two decades he spent many weeks of most years away from the British halls—unlike the majority of his colleagues who were primarily comedians and comic singers, but like such acrobats and dancers as the Martinettis, the Leopolds and the Lauris. For Little Tich, as for them, language had few barriers: his body spoke. As time went on he learned French, German, Spanish and Italian to help it out.

For at least ten years, from 1894 onwards, he is said to have made his home in Paris, as it was a convenient centre for his work. During this period, until 1904 at least, he stayed in a hotel when he worked in London. This indicates not only the internationalism of his status but his relationship to the British music hall; as does the fact that when he did move back to London with his second, Spanish-born wife (see chapter 9), much of the conversation in the family circle was conducted in French and Spanish. Although for most of the last quarter-century of his life his permanent address was a mansion block near the Oxford music hall, Little Tich never belonged to the variety world as did, say, Leno, Robey and Marie Lloyd. His sensitive awareness about his physical disabilities made him shun the busy public off-stage life in which his co-eminent contemporaries were usually to the fore: the Music Hall sports days, children's parties, old people's performances, charity galas, garden parties, outings, cricket matches, dances, banquets and sprees of one sort or another. He was, simply, not as gregarious as they were; he stood, to a degree, on his dignity; and as he felt himself a man apart, he kept apart (though he was privately generous in support of charities, good causes and deserving cases).

Soon after the start of his European career, Little Tich created the number which almost rivalled the Big Boot dance in popularity and which he described, indeed, as his 'greatest single-scoring success'. This was the 'Serpentine Dance', a parody of the skirt and scarf dancing of Loie Fuller. This American dancer might be described as a precursor of Maud Allan and Isadora Duncan in familiarizing music hall audiences with 'free' dance outside the conventional theatrical routines and balletic steps. When she introduced her dance to Paris at the Folies-Bergère in the autumn of 1892 (after appearing in Berlin, Altona and Cologne) 'she was lit by the very first electric footlights, installed especially for her'. The impact of her dancing was, in fact, partly due to the novelty of using electricity to such dramatic effect. According to Mistinguett, they called her the electric fairy: her act was a kind of Art Nouveau light show. She whirled tirelessly around the stage in spirals, her accordion-pleated skirts flying in layers picked out by the changing lights. And she caught the imagination of, among others, Toulouse-Lautrec with her serpentine, violet, butterfly and white dances.

In Berlin, Loie Fuller appeared in the same bill with Tich. According to him, it was she who first suggested that he should burlesque her. He was dubious; but she persisted, offering to lend him one of her dresses, and he was persuaded by the theatre manager and the editor of the *Berliner Tageblatt*. Tich took Miss Fuller's dress—a hundred yards of pleated gauze—home with him, only two or three hours before he was due to appear, and, as he put it, 'went to work with it before a mirror'.

> At the end of two hours my arms were aching, and all that I had managed to gather was that gauze silk was considerably heavier than lead, and that it had the most stubborn will of anything up to a donkey. Bless my soul! The more I tried to wave it the more knotted it got, and walking in sacks was nothing to it. You wouldn't believe the amount of natural sin there is in one of those serpentine skirts.

But when he did his take-off, immediately after Loie Fuller had finished her twirling, it was rapturously received; and it remained in Tich's repertory for years—as Little Miss Turpentine, or La Première Danseuse, or the Pet of the Opera, or the Pet of the Ballet. Usually the dance was enough, abroad. At home it was accompanied by a song, of which we give two verses.

> I'm the idol of London and Paris,
> I capture the biscuit with ease,
> I'm a dancer, you know, who is famous altho'
> I'm a little bit off at the knees.

60

My name is Virginia Harris,
Altho' I'm called Miss Turpentine
On account of the dance I brought over from France
In these dear little footsies of mine.

I'm the favourite danseuse of the Opera,
And the Czar never thinks me de trop.
Night and day, it is said, I'm on the King's Head,
That's the pub at the corner, you know.
I've a rival in Mademoiselle Liza—
Thinks she'll cut me out, but she won't.
She could never, you see, come within miles of me,
And I'll jolly well see that she don't.

'At the height of her serpentine prowess,' Sir Louis Ferguson
recalled, in *Old Time Music Hall Comedians*, 'something gave the
ballerina pause. With a vexed expression on her hitherto smirking
countenance, she stopped to pass yard after yard of muslin
through her fingers as though in a desperate quest. At last with
a grin of triumph she won through as far as her stocking and
scratched her leg. For this priceless moment you forgave all the
jokes on the subject of insect pests that had ever been perpetrated
on the Halls.'

The third number which, with Miss Turpentine and the Big
Boots, brought Tich especial fame abroad was his caricature of a
Spanish dancer. Like the other two, it depended for its success
almost entirely upon Tich's acrobatic, miming and dancing skills,
not upon songs or jokes. Parodying one of the sub-Otéros who
had proliferated in Paris since the 1890's—indeed, some critics
said that La Belle Otéro herself was the model—Tich bounced
round and round the stage with a monumentally large comb stuck
in a towering wig, wearing a spangled tutu, thrusting a rose in
his mouth, clicking his castanets with a demented intensity, dancing a fandango—and dancing it with precise expertise, despite the
comic business of getting mixed up with his mantilla. His ironic,
malicious smile gave a darker shade to the portrait. He was,
recalled Sacheverell Sitwell, 'sinister as well as funny': he resembled a picture by Zuloaga, 'though we may be sure that Goya
or even a greater and older name than he would have painted him.'
This was, as Jacques-Charles said, 'un cauchemar—mais un
cauchemar joyeux.' Pierre Bost, summing up Tich's career at his
death, said that in the Spanish number he achieved 'un style de

haute bouffonerie, concentré et definitif.' Tich had, in one sense, a definitive knowledge of Spanish dancers: he lived with one for nearly thirty years (see chapter 9).

Little Tich's Parisian career apparently began, almost accidentally, at the Folies-Bergère. He was offered a short engagement by the agent who supplied the Folies to do his Miss Turpentine number and the Big Boots dance. On the night of 11 December, 1896 Tich walked on unannounced, except as an extra turn. As one journalist said, 'he was immediately hailed as a genius of natural humour'. The Paris correspondent of the *Sunday Referee* reported two days later that no artist since Loie Fuller, four years earlier, had scored such a success. He was signed up for six months; and from then on, for the next decade, he was a star of Paris—a star, moreover, who was 'rediscovered' on at least one occasion. For two years he was at the Folies, but then he broke his engagement because of a counterbid by Joseph Oller of the Olympia; and the Folies' director, Edouard Marchand, brought a suit against Tich, claiming a large indemnity.

Although the French were the last to recognize him, Little Tich enjoyed working in Paris more than anywhere else outside London —and sometimes even more than inside London; or so it seemed on those occasions when he felt that his own countrymen were treating him (and his profession) with conspicuously less respect than did the French. To some sophisticated Parisians in the late 1890's Little Tich's appeal was partly due, as C. B. Cochran suggested, to the fact that he seemed to be 'the reincarnation of the dwarf court-jesters of the Middle Ages—the little English Don Antonio of Velasquez'. There before them, too, danced and capered the 'all licensed Fool' of Shakespeare. To others, in this Anglophile period, he seemed to be a Dickensian grotesque in the flesh. The influential novelist poet-critic, Jean Lorrain, extolled him in 1900 as a 'miraculous dwarf', a gnome escaped from one of Dickens's Christmas Tales; like a Daumier and a Guys at the same time; and, in 'drag' as a Spanish dancer, an animated 'Caprice' by Goya. He described him as:

Note Although Gustav Fréjaville dates Tich's Parisian debut as 1894, and even earlier dates have been suggested, it seems clear from a dozen other references in the press that it was, in fact, late in 1896/7. On Tich's return to Paris in 1923, he said that it was twenty-six years since he first appeared there at the Folies.

la grimace faite homme, l'humour dans la grotesque, le rire
et l'esprit dans la fantômatique, Little Tich, génial de laideur
et de souplesse étireé, avorton, effarant de contournements,
gobelin et farfadet qu'on se figure très bien jouant à saute-
mouton sur des comptoirs de bar qui seraient aussi des tombes;
et ce sont des gigues de Wite-Chapel et des pudeurs de M.
Prudhomme, cachant sous un chapeau son pied déchaussé et là-
dessus, des malices de lutin en goguette, des clignements d'yeux
complices, des redressements de tout son être et des prétentions
de petit homme à faire pouffer

Then, wrote Lorrain, Little Tich abandoned

sa silhouette de va-nu-pieds de Londres, sa redingote effrangée,
son pantalon en guenille et la prétention bien anglaise du
camélia qui fleurissait ses haillons : il aborde une étonnante
Espagnole, une frétillante et vertigineuse Manola de cauchemar,
qui sous ses longs accroche-coeurs se cambre, se déhanche, se
déclenche et se tortille et tout à coup, empêtrée dans sa mantille,
trébuche et s'étale par terre comme un pantin démantibulé; et
la Manola se relève, boitille sur des jambes tordues, et raide sur
ses reins anyklosés, la danseuse promène sur la scène la misère
grotesque d'un joujou faussé, jusqu'à la minute où gambillant
sur la musique, cette parodie de l'Espagne se remet à mimer
oeillades et sourires, et terrible comme une des planches des
'Caprices', véritable Goya animé, l'air à la fois d'un bouffon de
cour et d'une vieille duegne, elle tourne sur elle-même comme
une toupe humaine et disparait, s'évanouit, grotesquement
cambrée, fantastiquement hanchée, lubriquement hilare.

Harry Relph was embarrassed by the eulogies of Lorrain, often
quoted on Little Tich's visits to Paris twenty years later. It was
not only because of Lorrain's reputation as 'one of the most vicious
and dreaded reviewers in Paris', but because of his flagrant
homosexuality. Lorrain rouged and powdered his face, dyed his
hair red, used turquoise blue shadow on his eyes, loaded his fingers
with rings, picked up working class boys for one-night stands—
and made no secret of his sodomizing.

More to Harry's taste was the admiration of Toulouse-Lautrec.
The painter and the performer were almost of an age, and were
exactly the same height : four feet six. It is not known when
Lautrec first saw Harry's act; perhaps on his visit to London in
1894. But as an Anglophile and an habitué of the music halls,

he would have seen Tich for himself in Paris soon after Harry's 1896 debut there. They became friends for a few years before in 1899 the Count went into a mental home, an old man at thirty, 'always on the verge of delirium tremens, never sober, scarcely sane'. They were seen together in Paris and in Dieppe—where, so Walter Sickert told Sacheverell Sitwell—they frightened women on the pier by their deliberately offensive behaviour. Harry went to Lautrec's studio in the Avenue Frochot, and was invited to his chateau. Lautrec made at least one drawing of him—as a Spanish dancer, according to C. B. Cochran. This cannot now be traced, although Lautrec's portraits of several otherwise forgotten English performers—like May Belfort, May Milton and Cissie Loftus—survive; and no further detail of their relationship has been discovered. One painting from that period which *has* survived is by the Belgian artist Jan van Beers, who in 1898 sought out Tich in order to paint his portrait, partly (as he explained) because he wanted to capture on canvas the sitter's Punch-like smile. He painted Harry in his big boots, leaning forward, and signed it: 'To the great comic—Little Tich.'

Two of Little Tich's most eminent Parisian admirers were Lucien Guitry and his son Sacha. When Lucien was at the top of his profession, he used to make a point of coming to see Tich's act, night after night, when Tich was in Paris. The elder Guitry used to sit, it is said, in the front row of the stalls, leaning forward on his cane, watching Tich intensely—in quite a different way from the rest of the audience. He was, said Maurice Verne, taking lessons in humanity. Sacha was, perhaps, even more enthusiastic than his father, and his enthusiasm was no merely modish attitude, as it persisted for some thirty years. In 1907 we find Sacha saying to *Gil Blas* of Tich that 'il est impossible d'avoir plus de mesure et plus de tact dans la bouffonnerie'. In 1909, on a visit to England, he was quoted by the *Daily Telegraph* as saying, 'There is nothing I enjoy more than to spend an evening at the Tivoli in the company of artists like George Robey, Wilkie Bard and Little Tich. Shall I surprise you by saying that the last-named strikes me as the very embodiment of grace itself?' And Guitry later praised Tich for his inventiveness (witnessed by a thousand *drôleries* copied a thousand times since), his good taste ('Jamais une vulgarité, jamais une faute de goût'), his ability to make both the coarsest and the most cultivated members of the audience laugh at him and with him. Tich was, said Sacha, remarkable not

64

only as a performer but as an author, a director, a complete artist—and a gentleman.

Guitry's admiration was unflagging. In 1920 C. B. Cochran's 'Grande Saison Parisienne' in London was inaugurated by a reception given by Lady Cunard, the supreme professional hostess of the day, at her home in Carlton House Terrace. According to James Harding, Guitry's biographer, 'Sacha electrified the 400 guests by stating that his favourite actor was Little Tich, whom he described as the quintessence of art.' Lucien attended Tich's first night at the Alhambra when he returned to Paris in the 1920's. Henry Sherek, whose father booked the acts for that music hall and who sat next to Guitry, recalled in his reminiscences that:

> When Little Tich made his entrance, Guitry, dressed in his famous black cloak, jumped to his feet, turned to the audience, waved his broad-brimmed black-brimmed hat, and with something akin to madness in his voice shouted: 'Get up, all of you, in homage to the world's greatest genius.' This was perhaps a slight exaggeration, but to my surprise the audience did actually all get up and, led by Lucien, cheer for a considerable time.

This was not all, according to Sherek. Just when Tich thought he had finished his act Lucien Guitry bounced up in his seat and begged him to do the Big Boots dance, a plea in which he was loudly applauded again by the audience. While Tich, after some reluctance, went off to find the boots and put them on once again (he had rashly brought them, with no intention of using them in the act) Guitry harangued the audience about him. After the dance was over, Sherek says, 'Guitry kissed me on both cheeks and then rushed backstage and kissed Little Tich on both cheeks. To do this he had to kneel.'

For British music-hall performers it was a different climate in Paris. There was, for a start, far more of it going on than in London. When Tich first appeared in Paris there were 275 café-concerts, taverns, dance halls and other places where artists performed. It was also far *dirtier* than in London. According to the *Era*

> The stars, especially the female variety, nightly sing songs full of shocking allusions, suggestive details, accompanied by gestures which, far from exciting protestation, attract applause.

65

When he first appeared, Tich knew little of the language. The directors of the Folies made him promise that on his return visit he would sing one or two songs in French. He learned a couple, parrot-fashion, from Mme Violette, a *répétitrice* at the Folies, but endured such terrible stage fright on his opening night that he sang the second verse *after* the third. This, indeed, is said to have contributed to his success. Soon afterwards, he said, 'I did the best part of my entertainment in French, and felt gratified at my own efforts, until a friend of mine—one of the theatre-owning Isola Brothers—said, "Tich, you went extra tonight. They *love* an Irish accent in Paris." Within a year or two Tich sang fluently in French, with a very good accent; although his deliberate English interpolations and exclamations were prized by Parisians as part of his attraction (just as Footit's Yorkshire accent had been admired as an exotic addition to that English clown's funniness).

C. B. Cochran recalled, in one of his books of reminiscence, *A Showman Looks On,* that in Tich's 'debutante' number he would 'hurl himself' on to the stage, introducing himself—'Je m'appelle Clarice'—with a chuckle that, in retrospect, reminded Cochran of Edgar Bergen's ventriloquist's doll, Charlie McCarthy. In *Musées de Volupté* Maurice Verne attempted to record the phonetic effect of Tich's deliberately accented entrance lines in the following way:

Je m'epelle Clarisse. Je souis fille de un admiral . . . j'ai ete prisentai au bal de la cour . . . aoh, j'ai en beaucoup de sioucces . . . beaucoup de sioucces . . . very nice.

The 'very nice', as Cochran noted, was always in English. Verne describes how Tich's tiny figure, enveloped in a court dress with a long train and huge feathered fan, curtseyed with caricatured cere-monial grace, simpering meanwhile at the audience; then, suddenly, 'Clarice' was tripped up by her train, and, struggling to get it safely behind her and keep her dignity, shrieked 'Oh! charogne!', a local oath startlingly unsuited to an ad-miral's daughter at court. The voice suddenly changed; and, as Verne puts it, Clarice swore with a pure Parisian backstreet accent.

In 1904 Tich was among the first to appear at the Alhambra. Originally the Chateau d'eau Théâtre, it was turned by the British manager Thomas Barrasford into an English variety palace. During this season Tich routed one of his imitators, Little Pich, who had achieved some popularity in Paris during the past year with his version of the Spanish number and the Big Boots dance. 'When the real thing appeared,' one reporter noted, 'the Parisians recognized the genuine article and applauded him to the echo.' Tich consolidated his unique position in Parisian favour, reflected in a popular song of the time, 'Le pari de Little Tich,' and the fact that a local favourite, Dohmen, dubbed himself 'The Parisian Little Tich'. When he appeared in Paris in the following January, one critic declared that 'the big boots of Little Tich have left behind them their imprints on the sands of French variety business'. After his departure for Australia, a British journal reported that 'Little Tich is the music hall star possessing the greatest influence over the Parisian public, and commanding the highest salary.' On a week's visit to Paris the following year Tich was delighted to find that in three shows he visited—a play by Henri Bernstein, an operetta and an *opera buffe*—he was mentioned by name. As he told a Viennese interviewer laughingly, 'it makes me proud to have become a literary figure'.

The climax of Tich's success in Paris, before the first world war, came in 1904. He gave a professional matinee at the Moulin Rouge to thank his comrades of the Paris theatre for the welcome they had always given him. About 500 Parisian actors and performers from all branches of the theatre came. After his performance (entrance by invitation only) he was crowned with laurels and roses. He was presented with one laurel crown from the Gaieté theatre; another from M. Gémier and the Odeon; a jewelled gold cigarette case from Max Dearly; a statuette for him in costume from Senor Gauiraud; a pair of big boots in silver from Edmond Gideon; a silver smoking and writing service, incorporating a watch, from Guitry and the Renaissance Théâtre; a watch, chain and charm, representing the big boots, hat and cane, from the directors of the Moulin Rouge. Upwards of forty bouquets were thrown on to the stage. Coquelin and other leading members of the Comédie Française came to his dressing room to congratulate him. Afterwards he was the guest of honour at a special dinner. Tich was, understandably, overwhelmed.

I never felt so proud in my life, especially as I am a foreigner, and such a thing never happened to me in my own country.

He needed one thing only to complete his happiness in France. As he confided in a Parisian journalist, he had nursed a dream

67

for a long time which had not yet come true. 'You know how I love France. I want'—and Little Tich stopped, and sighed—like a child reaching for a coveted toy—'You're going to laugh at me, but I want les palmes académiques.' Six years later the dream did come true. In June 1910 the French Government bestowed on Harry Relph this order instituted by Napoleon and conferred on men of letters, scientists and 'all who advance education'. Little Tich was now an 'officer d'Académie', entitled to wear on ceremonial occasions an oval crown of two branches, palm and laurel, suspended by a violet ribbon from the left breast. For everyday use he could (and did) wear in his lapel a tiny violet rosette (often mistaken for the Légion d'honneur). He was, understandably, deeply proud of this decoration; all the more so because it honoured his art in a way that his own country had never done. Harry Relph, then forty-three, continued to work in Britain and abroad for nearly twenty years, with his artistry undimmed. Yet it remained unrecognized by one British Government after another. Although his friends George Robey and Harry Lauder were decorated in 1919, with a C.B.E. and a knighthood respectively, this was a recognition not of their brilliant talents as performers but of their labours as fund-raisers in the First World War. Tich himself, asked by the press to comment on Robey's C.B.E., was at first jocular (as was expected of him): 'Why all this fuss about new honours for the profession? Wasn't I created Lord Tom Noddy more than twenty years ago?' Then, more seriously, after expressing his personal delight that a 'very old friend' had been honoured, he voiced his disappointment that it was for Robey's 'great work' on behalf of war charities, not for his great work in the variety theatre. 'Why is it that a variety artiste is never singled out for distinction of this kind on his professional merits, while actors in the so-called legitimate and even managers in variety are considered eligible to have handles to their name?'

The knighted and baroneted variety managers, who had made fortunes out of the artists they employed, included Edward Moss —knighted as early as 1905—Oswald Stoll, Alfred Butt, and Walter de Frece who (with his wife Vesta Tilley) was Harry Relph's upstairs neighbour in Bloomsbury.

'This country,' Tich went on, 'is supposed to be more democratic than ever it was. Yet the line of demarcation between variety artistes and "actors" is, in this respect, drawn as rigidly as ever. No such division is made in France or in America. There

68

an actor is an actor, whether he plays Hamlet or wears the red nose and sloppy trousers of a vaudeville comedian.'

So far, so relatively safe: but Little Tich went further into forbidden territory, challenging long-entrenched cultural taboos.

'I maintain that on the score of individual ability the variety star is usually the better actor of the two. He has to do everything off his own bat, as it were, whereas the actor gets the support of his company. This makes a vast difference in the demand on the individual. Moreover, a variety star contributes individually much more to the general scheme of entertainment and the gaiety of nations. And I think it will be admitted that he enjoys, at least, an equal amount of popularity among his fellow-countrymen.

'It is time this unwritten law, this survival of snobbishness, was abolished. Because a man wears a grotesque make-up on the stage it doesn't follow that he will do or does anything derogatory to good taste or incompatible with a title . . . So long as an artiste offers wholesome entertainment he should be regarded as eligible for recognition whether he performs in a music hall or an opera house.' Half a century later nearly every official honours list in Britain annually hands out decorations to artists of the variety stage, working in the medium of television, irrespective of their 'wholesomeness' (by the standards of 1919) or their gender. But only one—George Robey—has been knighted since 1919.

In spite of the rare eminence that he achieved in France— recognized by the 1910 official honour—Little Tich did not return to the Paris stage between 1907 and 1923. Why? This is another of the mysteries about his life.

Why, when he was a prime attraction—even an idol—in Paris, when he was acclaimed and honoured there far more than in London, when he had perfected his French accent and his French-oriented act, did he not make the most of his power and glory there? Why, between 1907 and 1914 (after that, wartime considerations obviously intervened) did he ignore Europe— except for a week in Brussels? Instead of playing at the Folies or the Alhambra, why did he divide his working year—setting aside his South African tour—between London (the Tivoli, the Palace, and other halls), the suburbs (Hackney, Holloway, Shepherds Bush, etc.) and the provinces, moving—in the customary zigzag progress of the variety trouper—from Norwich

69

to Bristol, up to Newcastle, across to Manchester, north to Glasgow, down again to the Midlands in Nottingham, up to Liverpool, down south to Portsmouth and Brighton (a part of his itinerary in 1919). For somebody of Little Tich's eminence, there were three possible reasons why he should have deliberately absented himself from the felicity of Parisian acclaim for a third of his life. One is that, having virtually given up his Big Boots dance (see next chapter), he depended more upon the local colour of his character-numbers, and these were less readily exportable. This seems discounted by the fact that the absence of the Big Boots in the 1920's made little difference to his popularity in Paris; but Tich may have feared, from 1907 onwards, that it *would* make a difference—and he didn't want to damage the glory he had won. Another reason may be that Paris didn't *pay* enough. Tich needed a lot of money, which could be earned more easily (if such an artist's work can ever be described as 'easy') in the provincial variety palaces of Britain. Yet it seems likely that he could have got what he wanted in Paris, at this period. The third, and, we think, conclusive reason is that Tich *preferred* to work in his own country.

When Tich returned to Paris in October 1923, it was largely because he found it increasingly hard to get enough work in Britain. Although he was apprehensive about his reception at the Alhambra, after an absence of seventeen years, he need have had no fears. To many younger theatre-goers he seemed a major discovery: to those who had admired him before the war he seemed an even more remarkable artist. Although there was inevitably initial disappointment that he had dropped the Big Boots, several critics observed that this speciality had distracted their attention in pre-war days from the true quality of his work as an actor. Lorrain's romantic eulogies, which had passed into theatrical history, were found to be out of date. 'Fini le gnome terrifiant, et miraculeux: voici simplement un comédian originel et parfait, un grand artiste.' Moreover, Tich had himself mellowed and changed: according to Gustav Fréjaville, his make-up was much less extravagant—this critic remembered Tich in 1905 as having 'un visage violemment poussé à la caricature par un maquillage excessif'. There were, said Parisian connoisseurs, only two or three clowns of this kind in a generation. In his twenty-minute act, said René Bizet, you could see every comedian in one. The words 'greatness' and 'genius' were frequently invoked.

Then (and at his death) Tich was widely acclaimed in Paris as the true precursor of the early Chaplin. It was from Tich, said Bizet and others, that Charlie had taken the shuffling walk, the boots and the cane. Fréjaville affirmed that it was Tich who had invented on the stage most of the effects that Chaplin had re-created before the cameras: Charlie, he declared, owed Tich a good deal of his glory. He and others no doubt remembered Chaplin's imitation of Tich in 1909 when he appeared with the Karno Troupe during a month at the Folies-Bergère. Chaplin him-self never acknowledged any such debt. There is no mention of Little Tich in any study of his work—or in his autobiography: among the curious omissions from that book is the fact that he made his West End debut (at the age of eleven) in *Giddy Ostend* with Little Tich at the opening of the Hippodrome. Charlie's costume was apparently created in one afternoon, for *Kid Auto Races at Venice* in 1914, from the material to hand: oversize trousers from 'Fatty' Arbuckle, size 14 shoes from Ford Sterling (Chaplin wore them on the wrong feet, so that they wouldn't drop off), an under-size bowler and coat, a toothbrush moustache from Mack Swain, and a bamboo cane. In assembling this costume he was influenced, it seems, by his memory of the rag-and-bone man he had played in a Fred Karno sketch. Karno has, indeed, often been credited with a prime share in Charlie's paternity. Hal Roach said that as soon as Chaplin had 'exhausted the great material he had gathered over the years working for Fred Karno, then his pictures and he started to go down'. Part of that material was the example of Fred Kitchen, with whom he had toured in Karno companies. Kitchen was noted for his 'curious shambling walk, a cross between a shuffle and a hop', and for his big shoes: he claimed, indeed, 'to be the first comedian to wear outsize boots' (though Kitchen was still a child when Tich was on tour in *his* big boots). Although Kitchen does qualify for a mention in *My Autobiography*, Chaplin made no acknowledgement of gratitude or influence (however slight), any more than he did to Fred Karno, or Dan Leno, or others who may unwittingly have helped him to achieve his instant and amazing apotheosis as a universal comic. Yet it seems likely that in observing Little Tich's con-tribution to that sudden glory in mime, dancing and *style*, as well as boots and cane—French critics were more perceptive, here as elsewhere, than Tich's compatriots; and that, whether Chaplin realized it or not, the stock of technique and experience from

71

which he created the 'Little Fellow' included his memory of the seedy-elegant, cane-twirling, big-booted, character-acting, dancing manikin created by Harry Relph. When some younger Parisian theatre-goers in the 1920's wrote off Tich as a copyist of Chaplin, they ignored the fact that Tich was established—with boots, cane, et al—before Chaplin had learned to walk

After a highly successful season in 1923 Tich returned frequently to Paris before his death. He had, at a stroke, virtually re-established his old hold on the Parisian public, but in a new way: no small achievement for a British comic in his mid-fifties. A sure sign of his success came in the following spring when Sacha Guitry imitated him in 'La Revue de Printemps' (at the Théâtre de l'Etoile). It was about this time, perhaps, that Tich presented Sacha with a pair of his big boots, to add to a collection that included Napoleon's hat, Flaubert's dressing gown, Robespierre's waistcoat and Clemenceau's gloves.

When Little Tich died in 1928, the obituaries in the French press equalled—and, indeed, some surpassed—the British in their enthusiasm for his artistry. Pierre Bost, for instance, said that he found it very hard to decide whether, among the ranks of the great comics, Tich or Grock came first. Tich, moreover, has kept his place in the French pantheon of the music hall, where he is generally rated far higher than in its British counterpart. A typical verdict is that of the historian Serge, who described him in his *Histoire du Music Hall* (1954) as 'the greatest of all the eccentrics' and 'a comic genius'. Allowing for Tich's especial status as an exotic, it would seem that there has been a greater readiness among French critics and historians than among their British counterparts to take artists of the music hall at least as seriously as those of the straight theatre. Sacha Guitry said of Tich, back in 1922, 'Great comic acting, great comedy, should be recognised wherever it is found.' And the French seemed less surprised than Tich's fellowcountrymen to find it in the variety theatre. As the doyen of dramatic critics at the turn of the century, Sarcey, observed, Tich was 'un très grand petit artiste'. A British journalist in the *Star* commented at his death, 'To see Little Tich in Paris was to appreciate him in a way impossible in London. French audiences seemed to inspire him.'

7

FORTY YEARS AT THE TOP

> I am sole top of the bill—or not at all. There are only two artists
> I would ever share with—Little Tich and George Robey.
>
> Marie Lloyd, quoted by Clarkson Rose
> in *Red Plush and Greasepaint*, 1964.

For nearly forty years after his sudden rise to fame in 1890 Harry
Relph stayed at the top of the slippery pole of success in his
highly precarious, intensely competitive profession, out-living
almost all those other soloists with whom he had shared the
honours at the Pavilion and the Oxford in the first flush of his
stardom. As we have already indicated, he divided his working
life between variety theatres in London and the provinces; half a
dozen pantomimes in major regional cities (never in London, after
1894); frequent European tours between 1890 and 1906 and 1920
to 1927; and visits to America, South Africa and Australia. As a
veteran theatre journalist, H. G. Hibbert, put it, he was 'desper-
ately fastidious as to when and where and how he would work'—
and he was able to maintain that fastidiousness for many years,
at least until the mid-1920's. Soon after his rise to fame he set
his minimum price and stuck to it. In the 1890's it rose to £250
a week, and later to £300 (on occasion £400 in the provinces):
his total annual income seldom fell (until the 1920's) below
£8000 and often approached £10,000. He was very proud of
obtaining a nine-year contract for the Palladium at £300 a week.
And he must have gloried, privately, in being for a considerable
time one of the highest paid performers in Britain: not so
much because of what the money could bring but because of what
it symbolized to a man over a foot shorter than his competitors.
(Even Leno—at five feet three—stood nine inches above him.)

In spite of his social insulation from most of his fellow-per-
formers, Tich became more closely involved in the growing
organisation of the profession when he made London his base
around the time of his second marriage. About 1903 he joined
the Grand Order of Water Rats, which had been started fourteen

73

years earlier to promote Philanthropy, Conviviality and Social Intercourse among variety artistes; and he rose rapidly in the hierarchy, from Test Rat in 1903 and Prince Rat in 1904 to King Rat in 1906 (a post that Leno had held in 1891, 1892, and 1897). In 1903 he was elected a vice-president of the Music Hall Artistes Railway Association. Harry joined the Variety Artistes Federation on its formation in 1906, and was among the stars who supported the London music hall strike in the following year by helping to picket the offending theatres and refusing (or, rather, failing) to appear. He sent a telegram to the Tivoli, one of the 'blacked' houses, where he was top of the bill with Marie Lloyd, saying 'I am learning a new cornet solo. Cannot tear myself away.' (Marie Lloyd's telegram said, 'I am busy putting a few flounces on my dress so I cannot appear tonight.'). With Arthur Roberts and Joe Elvin he started an Emergency Relief Fund, to which hundreds subscribed.

As the years went by he saw such signs of the times as the refurbishing in 1900 of the 'Pav' in the style of Louis XV, in order—as the proprietors put it—'to cater for the growth of a public taste for art, elegance and luxury of appointments'; and, four years later, the first conversion of a big music hall (in Ardwick, Manchester) into a cinema—though for more than a decade after the cinematograph appeared in 1896 silent films were (via the Bioscope) given house room in music hall bills, a mark of that all-embracing eclecticism which was one of the splendours of 'variety' at its best, and which, although it may once have seemed lethal in causing the subjugation of soloists like Tich by package-deal shows, ephemeral crazes and novel gimmickry, is the abiding reason for its persistence as a main pillar of the truly national theatre. Tich himself was never taken up by the impresarios of the new technology, although he was seen on the screen as early as 1900 in Paris at the Great Universal Exposition, where in the Photo-Cinéma-Théâtre a fashionable photographer, Clément Maurice, also showed films of the clowns Footit and Chocolat; and he appeared briefly in a Méliès film of 1905, 'An Adventurous Automobile Trip'.

Tich worked through the long struggle with the 'legitimate' theatre managers over the performance of 'straight' drama, and saw in 1912 the pyrrhic victory of the music halls when they won official sanction for their staging of dramatic sketches. He saw the extension of variety's frontiers to include not only one-act plays but potted opera, *scènes de ballet,* spectacle, and mini-tragedy, with such artists as Bernhardt, Beerbohm Tree, Yvette Guilbert and Nijinsky. He saw the rise and decline of the 'theatre of varieties', the network of Empires, Palaces and Hippodromes, with their gilt, plaster and red plush, largely controlled by the two Northern impresarios, Moss and Stoll: a network still expanding after the boom in film business. He saw the enthronement of respectability, symbolized by the growth of royal patronage. This was initiated by Edward VII, who watched Leno privately at Sandringham and went publicly to the Empire and Alhambra, but was sealed by George V with the first Royal Command performance in 1912 at the Palace Theatre. (Tich sang 'Popularity', a 1910 number, and did his Big Boots dance, but was too nervous to appear in the grand finale.) He saw, in the wake of ragtime and jazz, the disappearance of the exploitable song-writer, who instead of being content to take £5 or at most £10 by selling exclusive rights to a star like Tich, chanced his arm in the market where he might earn hundreds, even thousands, from a 'free' song. And Harry saw the advance of revue, which after its first spasmodic vogue in the 1890's was—in the first twenty years of the new century—to transform the working lives of soloists like himself more radically than did the competition of the silent film.

In 1902 Tich starred, with Marie Lloyd, in a Coronation Revue at the Tivoli, appearing as a prehistoric man, Ben Hur and Faust (sending up his friend, the tenor Jean de Reszke), with Marie Lloyd as his Marguerite (she also played Bernhardt). Reporting on this show the *Music Hall and Theatre Review* observed, 'There is fashion in the halls as elsewhere, and it looks very much as if reviews were coming in like Panamas.' Tich, in fact, came out of this revue after a week (with Marie Lloyd), because of disagreements with the management; it ran only for a month, as part of the music hall bill; and Tich declared that he would never play in revue again. But within a few years this form—combined in the bill with single turns—became popular at the Empire and Alhambra; and by 1914 the Hippodrome, Palace and Middlesex had gone over completely to revue. The *Era* declared in that year that revue was 'firmly established as the staple entertainment of the larger houses.' At the Tivoli, Pavilion and Oxford the single turn was still, as the *Era* pointed out, the 'mainstay' of the entertainment; but in the same year the Tivoli

75

closed down, and the Oxford went over to musicals and plays. In 1918 the Pavilion, too, surrendered to revue, under Cochran's direction. Soloist variety—the realm of Little Tich—endured in his lifetime at the Palladium (till 1922), the Victoria Palace (till 1928) the Coliseum (till 1930) and the Holborn Empire (till 1940).

In 1916 Tich said that, although he had 'set his face against the revue for so long', he had now agreed to join the cast of *Flying Colours* at the Hippodrome (that theatre paid the Palladium £100 a week for the privilege of engaging him). Tich took the decision, he said, mainly because it was the only way of staying for more than six or seven months a year in and around London, as individual turns were now practically 'squeezed out'. A job in revue would mean six times as much work and no more money, said Tich, 'but I am prepared to make the sacrifice'—in order to have from six to ten months at home. If this was, indeed, his intention, it was a miscalculation; *Flying Colours* ran for only four months; and Tich left it after less than three months, in order to work in a Glasgow pantomime (with the new woman in his life: see chapter 11). He worked in no more revues after *Flying Colours*. During the next six years he was, in fact, never away from London and suburban dates for longer than twelve weeks (including pantomime engagements). From 1923 onwards, however, he found it hard, he said, to get more than four or five months work in Britain; and when he did so in London he had sometimes to accept second place on the bill—at the Coliseum, for instance. Felix Barker, the Coliseum's historian, records that: 'He was quick to make a joke of the indignity. 'Oh dear,' he confided to the orchestra at one rehearsal, 'It's the early worm that gets the bird!' During this period the Coliseum—one of the few theatres in central London still engaging single turns—featured at their expense such novelties as tennis: in 1924 half the bill was given over to four professionals demonstrating shots against a backcloth of the Centre Court at Wimbledon, and knocking autographed balls into the audience. Moreover, Tich was often obliged to appear three times a day—a practice which started at the Palladium in wartime. As early as 1906 Tich had attacked this managerial trend because 'it simply meant for the performer a monotonous life of "from bed to work and from work to bed." Two performances a day were quite sufficient physical strain.' Moreover, said Tich, attendances at matinees were often un-

76

economically sparse; and it was an additional strain for artists to attempt to galvanize a scatter of customers into an audience—what's more, a *laughing* audience. In wartime, however, the boom in music hall business dissolved that obstacle, though the other objections remained. And Tich was working three times a day in the last year of his life.

The general pattern of Little Tich's solo act was already set by 1890, when he first became famous, and persisted until his last appearance in 1927. This is not to say that he ceased to develop as an artist, or that he went on singing, dancing and clowning in the same hit-numbers and the same style that took him so quickly to the top. On the contrary, notices from discerning observers on both sides of the Channel (allowing for Parisian hyperbole in this respect) prove that as time went by he refined his act, enlarged it, perfected it. He was never content to rest on his laurels. Every year he added new songs and new characters, jettisoning earlier ones en route. His artistry mellowed and diversified. His humour—as Parisian observers pointed out in the 1920's—became gentler, more subtle, less grotesque (reflected in the reduced exaggeration of his make-up and costume); though it was no less fantastic in its inventiveness and accurate in its satire at the end of his career than at its beginning. But the shape and appeal of Tich's performance were, substantially, the same for nearly forty years.

The three main structural elements in Tich's act were—as in many other variety acts—the song; the dance; and the character. In trying to understand his especial expertise, it is almost impossible to distinguish between those elements: mainly, of course, because he's been dead for fifty years, but partly because those elements were not (as in many other acts) separate, marketable turns. The song and dance were both, indivisibly, part of the character; no matter that he (or she) lived for only three minutes a night. And the character—caricatured, of course, though it was—usually had an intense reality, energized not so much by social observation and experience but by Tich's own irreducible, irresistible mana, charisma, call it what you will: by the drive, moreover, of a man with a natural disposition to side with the underdog against the normal-height, normally fingered, normally-talented majority.

First, the songs. About fifty of at least 140 songs survive in manuscript in his daughter's keeping; over thirty recordings are

77

listed in a discography by Tony Barker of which fewer than a dozen are preserved, on disc, in the archives of the BBC and the British Institute of Recorded Sound. We should acknowledge, from the start, that none has passed into the popular repertoire of old-time favourites. As numbers on their own, they are forgotten; they may well remain, as songs, buried in oblivion. But in Tich's time—and it was a great time—they were indispensable in helping him to create the characters on whom he largely depended in his act, as was the case with Leno, whose songs are equally obliterated by history. Tich's prime triumphs did not depend on words at all; but between the peaks were the songs, bought—before World War I for a fiver or at most a tenner—as his exclusive property. 'Authors and composers get to know one's style,' Tich explained in an interview in 1907, 'and they send 'em along. If one strikes me as being good, I buy the song right out, and then try it, and as a rule it goes dead. Oh! It's a fine sinking fund, buying songs for the public to listen to. You are very lucky if you get one decent song out of six.' A few years later you were lucky indeed to get one to yourself at all: authors and composers wrote directly for the public and the publishers, not for the performers. In 1920 Tich was complaining that 'most of the authors will not trouble to write an exclusive song for one man. They make more money in writing free songs.' Yet he was still able at the very end of his career in 1926/7 to buy for £5 the sole singing and performing rights in songs—though half the fees and royalties were assigned to the songwriter 'in the event of publication, or reproduction'.

'In regard to songs', said Tich in his ghosted autobiography, in one of the few passages, his daughter says, which bears the imprint of his personality, 'there are several things to consider. You see, I have six kinds of songs, viz:

1. Songs I have sung with success;
2. Songs I have sung;
3. Songs I have not sung;
4. Songs I never intend to sing;
5. Songs I daren't sing;
6. Songs . . .'

He sang them swiftly with a chirpy, energetic, attacking charm, in a light, precise, rather high voice. Among the most characteristic of the surviving songs is a number from the 1890s (in the

78

Charles Chilton collection): 'I'm an Inspector' with words by Harry Wright and music by Fred Eplett (who wrote and composed many of Leno's songs) dates from 1895: it was published in *Sheard's Comic Annual*, 1896. Like all Tich's character-songs, it clearly depends for its effect on the height of the singer. *Bus.* stands for comic business i.e., the life-blood of the act.

A most determined man am I, a man of brain and muscle
I'm never hasty, no not me, I'm never in a bustle
Cool and calm I always keep with firm determination
My word is law whene'er I speak to my men in the station.
My orders only given once are instantly obeyed
My men all know the consequence when orders are delayed.

Spoken: Rather, they know better than to contradict me, Why I have my men so completely under my thumb (business with thumb), that one word from me makes them do exactly as they like. Why, if I look at them they tremble, but if I glare at them they fly as though they were shot. When I'm in a temper I think nothing of picking up a constable in each hand, giving them a good shaking and throwing them in the corner like pieces of tissue paper. Ah, they can't come any of their tricks with me, because . . .

Chorus: I am an inspector
It really seems my duties never cease
Early or late, quite up to date,
I'm an inspector of the Metropolitan P'lice.

I can't be square, well hardly so, or lose my head to beauty.
I never notice women's tears, I always think of duty.
Do as you'd like to be do'ed is always my contention
Act fair and square, that's when you can, to that please pay attention
That I have got a master mind it's easy to discern
My temperament, you all can see, directly I look stern.

Spoken: Do you observe that look? Two of those looks are warranted to stop any clock. Many a hardened ruffian who has fought and killed 20 policemen at one blow, has quailed and even begged for mercy when I've looked at him like that. Now just to show you the marvellous magnetic influence of my wonderful eye; only the other day a carriage and a pair of horses ran away and what did I do eh? What did I do! (*bus.*) Why, I ran

D

into the middle of the road like that. (*bus.* running) I always run like that. I looked at 'em—quite sufficient—they immediately turned round and walked back to where they had started from. But that's nothing. I only *have* to look at a public house and it loses its licence.

'I'm An Inspector' belongs to a long line of character-songs stretching over more than thirty years. Dozens of men (and a few women) were featured by Little Tich in their jobs. Many of these numbers were topical and most were ephemeral, disappearing after a year or two; but some of perennial appeal and comic resilience were revived and refurbished every now and then. The list of known characters begins in 1884 with a waiter and included the following in roughly chronological order: policeman, sailor, soldier, lifeguardsman, artilleryman, lamplighter, mandarin, fireman, bandmaster, bus conductor, chef, cricketer, tram conductor, pugilist, big game hunter, war correspondent, pirate, dandy, toreador, park-keeper, cavalryman, draper, gas inspector, pier master, General, bargain hunter, barber, polar explorer, dentist, zoo keeper, doctor, gamekeeper, bargee, steeplejack, 'seaside skipper', skating rink instructor, drill sergeant, tallyman, railway porter, tax collector, huntswoman, schoolboy, farmer, debutante, lost property man, gendarme, barrister, Frenchman in London, school-master, MC at the *palais de danse,* gladiator, skivvy, butcher's boy, blacksmith, grocer, cook and charlady. This is not a comprehensive list; and several of these occupational characters were, not surprisingly, featured by other soloists like Leno. But this part-inventory—'a series of daft miniatures', as J. B. Priestley has called them—indicates the range of Tich's instant characterization; for each creation was individually distinctive not only in make-up and costume, but in movement and presence. Not only the song but the dance changed from person to person, and although they were outlined in no more than thumbnail sketches, they were usually more than grotesques. As Sir Neville Cardus said, he was—like Robey, Wilkie Bard or Harry Tate—'a comic actor, with a keen eye for character'; and he was 'essentially serious: the laughter he caused came as a by-product of his impersonating art'.

Many of the songs were written by Alf Ellerton (words) and Will Mayne (music) but Tich himself wrote a number of his own songs: the words, music *and* orchestral arrangements.

80

A gifted musician, Tich not only enjoyed playing the cello at home, and sometimes—to the favoured few, like Cicely Court-neidge—in his dressing-room; but he was also held in unusually high professional esteem by theatre conductors and players. At his death George Saker, the Alhambra conductor, who had worked with Little Tich for twenty years, said:

> He was more meticulous than any other star I have ever known, but no man showed more consideration for the orchestra. Unlike many other stars who send their dressers to Monday morning rehearsals he invariably turned up in person, and his band parts were always neat and in order. If necessary he would sort them out himself, and during the rehearsal would suggest how certain numbers should be accompanied. He understood music. Any conductor with whom he worked will tell you that he never let an orchestra down.

Excavators among Tich's songs may find revealing reminders of an England before the National Health Service and the welfare state: as in Tich's story as a tallyman of the lady who obtained a set of artificial teeth by paying five shillings down and fourpence every Good Friday. 'And the first time I asked for payment she bit me—with my own false teeth.' The songs are veined with a nursery surrealism. As a zookeeper Tich had been friendly with the elephant, he confided to the audience, until Jumbo drank his beer. But he got his own back by waiting till the elephant was asleep, and then eating all Jumbo's hay. As a gamekeeper, he revealed, 'When I know poachers are about I employ a strategy. You see, I've got an arrangement with an old buck rabbit. I give him the tip when there's any shooting on, and when poachers are about he lets me hide down his burrow.' And as a lost property man he described his store with 6000 umbrellas, and twenty-four glass eyes gazing on the wooden legs hanging all around. Apart from the fantasy and nonsense, there is a plethora of puns, chestnuts and vintage jokes in the old music hall tradition of the cleaner kind.

Here is a number dating from 1910, when the Territorial movement was in the news. It achieved a longer life than many of Harry's songs, for it was one of those music hall numbers chanted on the roads to hell four years later by the 'Old Contemptibles'. It began

I am a bolger sold—I mean that I'm a soldier bold,
I'm not so young as I used to be, before I got so bold;
I am a reckless dog, I am, I am, I say I am,
But you can't tell what's inside the jar by the label on the jam!

Then came the chorus, which gave the song its appeal to the troops

I'm a soldier, a Territorial,
The girls all say when I'm on parade
'There's one of the Boys of the old Brigade'.
Whenever I go to war,
I drive the enemy barmy
Hi, hi! Never say die!
I'm one of the Deathless Army.
Hi, hi! Never say die!
I'm one of the Deathless Army.

Here is one from 1919, by Alf Ellerton, belonging to the more sophisticated part of Tich's repertoire: 'The Barrister'.

Verse You've heard of Truthfuss Highsocks, well, I am that legal toff,
    My fee's one word a guinea, and it's five pounds when I cough.
    A lawyer with a conscience, which I never bring to Court,
    I'm great at breach of promises, and cases of that sort.
    So, girls, if you want damages, just call and bring my fee,
    Put yourselves right on my hands and leave the rest to me.

Chorus The law—ah, ah—it's very peculiar,
    Justice is blind, with lawyers at the Bar.
    And when to Law for damages you go,
    You're the one that's damaged, while the barristers get the dough.

Patter (addressing the conductor as the judge): My Lord, I am pleading for a separation order on behalf of a wife. They cannot agree, only to disagree. My client asserts she has been struck. Her husband asserts that his wife has also struck him. I'll admit he has come to court to show you his bad back, I'll admit his back is bad, but there are faults on both sides. They married and had children, 1909, in May. He was seen to have several drinks, 1910, in July. And was seen to kiss his housemaid several times, 1911. The
82

wife has an intense longing for a dish known as bubble and squeak. The husband cannot bear the dish—in fact, he squeaks every time he hears it bubbling. I ask for a separation for incompatibility—incompatibility of bubble and squeak. Granted! Exit wife bubbling, exit husband squeaking.

This is one of the characters in which Neville Cardus, writing in 1967 in the *Guardian,* particularly remembered Little Tich; but it was not the song that stayed in his memory. Cardus wrote, indeed, 'I can't remember that he ever sang; yet he must have sung.'

Tich nearly dropped this number in its first week after he introduced it at the Alhambra in 1919 because, he told Win, later the third Mrs Relph, 'I cannot get the right finish.'

When I reassured him, Harry answered, 'You overestimate my capabilities.' But it was the very next afternoon that he greeted me with the exclamation, 'I've got it. And it was a riot!' On the spur of the moment he had tried to lift a huge tome—a prop on the 'legal' table—but the unexpected weight caused him to stagger backward instead of going forward. The pantomime of trying to keep his balance with ludicrous footwork, finally losing control of feet, book and dignity, sent the audience into hysterical laughter, and of course the nonsense work provided him with the perfect means of getting off stage.

Tich's very last song (see chapter 14) should be recorded here: not because of the merits of its lyrics, but because it helped to kill him, prematurely. Arthur Martyn wrote the words; we can find no record of the composer, but maybe it was Tich himself. It was called 'The Charlady'; and the special thing about her was that she 'did' for the House of Commons ('I'm Parliament's Queen'). Here is one of the verses, followed by part of the patter and the chorus. The text is taken from Mr Martyn's manuscript, preserved in Tich's files; we don't know how much of the patter he used or how closely he followed the script, but this gives a picture of Tich's verbal material at the end of his career—and of his life.

Verse   In the Lobby I dance
       When I get half a chance

They call me the Charing Pavlova.
But one day I got hurt
For I tripped in my skirt
And I skid (sic) on the soap and fell over.

Patter I know all the MPs. Mr Baldwin and I are very pally. He came up to me the other day and he said, 'Mrs Catchpole?' I said, 'Yes, Stan.' He said, 'What do you think we ought to do about China?' I said, 'Smash it.' He said, 'But I can't.' I said, 'Well, if you can't smash it, sit on it!'

Lloyd George came in one day and he said, 'Mrs Catchpole, this is St David's Day, and I have a leek in my buttonhole.' I said, '*Have* you? You ought to go and see a plumber.'

Then there's Winston Churchill. The other day he took me in a corner of the Lobby and showed me his Budget! He said, 'I've got two hundred million pounds here.' I said, 'Have you! Come on. Let's go down to Margate.' He said, 'You've got to have a brilliant head for this job.' I said, 'Yes, but I'll tell you how you can make *yours* more brilliant still.' He said, 'How?' I said, 'Use Ronuk.'

Then there's Ramsay Mac. Now, there's a nice man. The only thing I don't like about him is his moustache. Every time he has a plate of soup he has to squeeze it out. He's Scotch—I'd sooner have him out of a bottle.

Mind you, I like my job. I like cleaning the statues in the Lobby. You *do* get among the 'heads' so. One day I'm soft-soaping Gladstone, another day I'm whitewashing Disraeli. But I got in a row the other morning when I was doing Campbell Bannerman. I knocked two of his buttons off and scrubbed the crease out of his trousers! . . .

Chorus A Charlady am I,
I'm one of those who char.
Though I'm not in the public eye
I get in the Public Bar.
I scrub and polish all day long
I've always sundry jobs on
But I've not yet got
Those housemaids' knees with knobs on.

Tich's 'business' for the charlady included a moment when he stood on the end of his mop. One night in 1927 (see chapter 14) the mop failed to achieve what it was supposed to do. The handle shot up and hit Tich smartly on the side of his head. And that was the end of a great performer.

Neither the song nor the patter was of prime importance in Tich's work. Among his most eminent (and his most eloquent) admirers is J. B. Priestley, who wrote in 1929, the year after Tich's death, that none of the national losses of 1928—Haig, Hardy, Asquith—had troubled him more than the loss of Little Tich. Yet, Priestley then said, 'his songs mattered not at all. You hardly ever caught the words of them, and when you did you found you had been listening to no purpose. The matter of his songs and talk was the old traditional stuff . . . an ancient round of japes. But all this was mere fodder for the unsophisticated, bait for the groundlings. On a far higher level were his actions, his sudden gestures.' Forty years later, in *Particular Pleasures*, Priestley was less dismissive: 'There were usually songs of a sort, sung at a frantic speed, delivered to you as if they were so much routine rubbish, perhaps a minor item in a contract. And anyway you were still laughing at the sight of him.' It was when he *stopped* singing, said Priestley, that 'his drolleries were inspired and irresistible'.

Certainly it was not by his songs that Little Tich made his name and kept it—or by his jokes. As one admirer said, 'Why should a man with such a laugh trouble to make good jokes? Apparently he knows that a good laugh is better than any joke. He rarely makes the mistake of offering you a really good joke. He knows that you're more likely to laugh (with his assistance) at a poor one.' He gave as an example the chestnut, 'What is a honeycomb? The thing people go on when they're married.' To read that ancient quip is to be amazed that it could ever be exhumed on the stage by a twentieth century star. But, according to this witness, 'as said by Little Tich, it can make a thousand people laugh and laugh again'.

How does he do it? He has no eyebrows to assist him. His nose is genuine. His hat is not abnormal. His clothes might pass in the street. Quite simply. Gravely he puts the question. And he replies in this way. 'The thing (*he begins to laugh*)— that people go on (*he continues to laugh*)—when they're (*he becomes almost speechless with laughter*)— married' (*entirely*

85

doubled up with laughter). And his laughter infects the whole theatre. You lose sight of the joke and see nothing but Little Tich, completely overcome.

Even when you couldn't *hear* the laughter, but saw it shaking him from head to foot as he tried to suppress and silence it, the infection spread. Then it would suddenly explode in a whistle of laughter, 'like a jet of steam from a boiler under pressure.'

It was not just a mastery of infectious laughter-making, however, that distinguished Tich for so many years. There were scores of comic singers at work in Tich's lifetime, and many other 'eccentric' acrobatic clowns, but none combined—in quite the way that he did—song, mime and dance. As a dancer he was in a class of his own; and his highly individual use of movement —his instant skips, gambols and leaps, as well as his expert performance of tap, soft shoe, and Spanish dancing—was a most important element in his persistent popularity. 'When Tich doth dance,' wrote Harry Graham, 'I wish he might do nothing else. Every form of Terpsichorean art comes naturally to his nimble feet.' He was capable of extreme rapidity, mobility and agility, with a kind of sudden-ness that took the audience by surprise. 'We talk of people breaking into a dance, but the verb flatters them,' J. B. Priestley wrote after his death. 'Little Tich, however, really did break into a dance, fifty fantastic little steps, and out of it again almost before you knew what was happening.' According to Sir Sacheverell Sitwell, 'Valentin-le-desossé of the Moulin Rouge may have been his only rival;' and Sir Osbert Sitwell said (in *The Scarlet Tree*) that Tich was 'surely a dancer of genius'. It is noteworthy that whenever Nijinsky came to London with the Diaghilev ballet (according to Sir Sacheverell) he asked to be taken to see 'Little', as he called Tich—because he regarded him as a master of dancing (and make-up, too).

When the ballet-master and choreographer Eddie Espinosa first saw Tich in action, he hurried round backstage afterwards to discover who had taught him such unusually expert and versatile technique. Tich was, in fact, entirely self-taught. He had been learning for himself since childhood. One of his early successes in the 1890s was a number he wrote himself (with music by George Ison) called 'I Really Can't Stop Dancing':

I've always had a mania since the day that I was born
To study up the art of Terpsichore.

86

I was fairly dancing mad, and I'd practise night and morn
And jump and shuffle on my kitchen floor.
My mother often walloped me for making such a row
And swore that she would cure me of my prancing,
But when I saw her going for me, I'd dodge away somehow
And all day long I'd never leave off dancing.

Chorus   Dancing, don't I love to pirouette
        It makes me feel so gay, I could keep it up all day
        It is my greatest pleasure, you can bet
        To me it is entrancing
        I'm dancing when I'm eating, or when I laugh or cry,
        I cannot break myself of it, no matter how I try,
        I'm dancing when I'm sleeping, I'll be dancing when I
          die,
        I really can't stop dancing.

The dance for which Tich was best remembered was the one he
liked the least. It was his own peculiar speciality—although, as
we have seen, he did not invent it, and although many people tried
to imitate it. According to the novelist H. E. Bates, (in *The
Vanished World,* 1969) Tich's boots were made—for a time, at
least—in Higham Ferrers by his grandfather, George William
Lucas, 'a craftsman of the highest class', who liked to claim that
he had made not only the largest shoes in the world but also the
smallest (for a midget dancer). The Big Boots dance originated,
as we described in chapter 3, in Tich's blackface period and the
popularity of clog dancing in late Victorian music hall. It was a
grotesque blend of the soft shoe and the sand dance, which began
softly and worked up to a crescendo, with one wooden sole after
the other noisily slapping the stage. But the popularity of the
number was due more to Tich's acrobatic and juggling skills, and
to his comic genius, than to his talents as a dancer. He would
juggle with his top hat: balancing it on the edge of his chin,
making it somersault and catching it on a boot, or his chin, or
his nose. He would use the boots as stilts or crutches, or rattle
them like bones. There was no song, no patter, no funny clothes.
One of its conspicuous features was the *lean*: Tich discovered
that he could lean forward almost horizontally with straight legs
and then raise himself back to the upright position, either slowly
or with dazzling rapidity. He used this to pick his hat or cane
off the floor: to pretend to fall, to swim—or to fly; to take a bow.

He also developed the *slide*—doing the splits sideways, fast or slow, while keeping his legs perfectly straight. This was possible because he had developed not only strong leg muscles, but because of the balance created by the solidity of the boots and the fact that they were in length half his own height. In its best-known form, the Big Boots number was danced to music written especially for him by a leading French composer and conductor, Auguste Bosc, creator of the Bal Tabarin and a personal friend; and this lively, bouncy schottische became something of a signature tune which was often played in his heyday by the orchestra in a restaurant or theatre when Little Tich was known to be present. Tich's boots were so famous by the mid-1890s that they appeared in children's comics, advertisements and the slot-machines of seaside piers. When you put in a penny, the effigy of Tich raised his top hat and leaned forward at an angle of forty-five degrees.

For some twenty years the Big Boots dance was regarded as an indispensable part of Tich's turn. As far back as 1896 he aroused the hostility of an Edinburgh audience when he failed to give the number on a Monday night opening. As the *Edinburgh Evening News* reported:

> Answering loud cries for an appearance in his fantastic boots, he explained that one of them had been broken on Saturday, and that he had not yet had it repaired. The explanation being received with derision, Little Tich walked off the stage . . . The curtain was rung up on a pair of comedians, who had to retire from the torrent of whistling and encoring which pursued Little Tich. A coster comedian next appeared, but he too was denied the semblance of a hearing, and the curtain finally fell on a discreditable scene. The cheaper parts of the house emptied themselves slowly and noisily, with shouts of 'Give us back our money.'

There were somewhat similar scenes in several cities when he decided in his mid-forties to give up the Big Boots for good. Tich was so indignant at the barracking he received at the Nottingham Empire, on this account, that he swore as he left the stage that he would never come to Nottingham again. He never did.

Tich hated the enormous popularity of this number because it obliged him to repeat over and over again something that was, in his view, no more than a grotesque novelty number that, like

88

all novelty numbers, should have been discarded when it ceased to be new. It was, moreover, exhaustingly hard work. After a bad fall in Belfast in 1909 Tich gave up dancing on the tips, and a few years later, about 1915, he gave it up altogether in Britain, reviving it on only one or two special occasions. One of these was the occasion when his little daughter was watching him with her mother from a box at the Coliseum, and he donned the Big Boots as a surprise treat for them both, as they had never seen him do it. Soon afterwards the manager brought a message to Tich's dressing-room from Sir Oswald Stoll asking him to continue doing the number in his act. Tich sent back the following reply: 'Please convey my compliments to Sir Oswald, and tell him that if he would like to pay me another hundred a week I shall be pleased to do the Big Boots.' Tich knew he was safe. When he omitted to do the Big Boots number on his second Australian tour of 1926/7, pennies were thrown on the stage by a boorish audience in Adelaide—and Tich, in disgust, abandoned the tour. But he sometimes revived this speciality on Continental dates at the end of his life, under pressure from the management. When he put the boots on for the first time in a decade, while working Budapest in 1925, and kept them on for three shows in a day, he had to spend the next day in bed because his legs were so painful—'until I get into training,' as he wrote to his mistress.

Some admirers were glad when he gave up the boots. As a *Manchester Guardian* critic said: 'he threw away what had seemed a crutch, and we found that he had not been leaning on it as hard as we thought. And he goes on throwing away other things: what was a great success a year ago is done with today, and we find him relying on something entirely new. Or perhaps that is expressing it quite wrongly, for it is not on these appurtenances, old or new, that he relies. There is something fundamental in him which would make anything "come off." '

As J. B. Priestley said of the boots, 'after all, they were just a gimmick, and he remained a great comedian, without any help from them'.

Why and how was Tich a 'great comedian'? What was it, apart from his dancing, that made both British and French connoisseurs, uncorrupted by instant show business idolatries, say that he was touched with genius? To such questions there are no easy answers. We shall attempt to summarize the factors in Tich's achievement in a final chapter. But first, let us take another look at

Tich in action, as described by the artist Paul Nash in *Outline*.

The scene tonight was a familiar one—a street with a background of houses and trees. On the right hand wing, a corner house with an area and a grating. Tich has on his fantastic boots and his little comic hat and he waves and waggles his little swagger cane. With this equipment he can make you laugh and can fascinate you endlessly with his nimble dancing and his twittering songs. Presently he will inadvertently hit his long boot with his cane, and his surprise and pain will be unbearably funny. Suddenly he sees the grating. At once the gay, innocent comic becomes a mischievous little monster, all leers and terrible chuckles. Turning his back he leans over his boots—which is funny enough in itself—he peers through the grating and begins to show signs of naughty excitement, his little stick held casually behind his back somehow begins to look like a little dog's tail which begins to wag with pleasure. The audience is not slow to get all these signs and they laugh and hoot and whistle rude whistles. Tich is delighted with his peep show and, as the band begins to play its catchy tune again, he begins to sing.

> Curi-uri-uri-osity, curiosity,
> Most of us are curious
> Some of us are furious,
> I do think it's most injurious
> Curious to be.
> What did I get married for?
> Curiosity.

After this Tich makes some patter, and when the chorus breaks out again there is a crescendo of laughter and applause. Tich becomes tremendously animated and does a wonderful little dance, slapping his boots together in mid-air.

Paul Nash prefaced this account of 'the incredible Little Tich', which mixed separate numbers into one composite impression, by contrasting the public Tich, 'an expression of comic genius', with the private man, 'rather grave and inclined to studiousness'. It is now time to turn to that private world of Harry Relph off the stage.

90

PART TWO

PART TWO

8

THE FIRST MRS TICH

Harry maintained throughout his life a marked respect and admiration for women. He would never permit men to swear in a lady's presence when he was around; nor would he permit discourtesies of any kind to be said or shown: not even a harsh word about those who had done him wrong, however angry or hurt he may have felt.

Mary Tich

Harry Relph made a small fortune by being conspicuously small, and by encouraging audiences to laugh at his physical peculiarity. Yet, inside himself, he apparently never came to terms with his disabilities. According to his third wife, 'he would have given up stardom, anything, if he could have been the height of other people'. He was exceptionally alert to any suspicion that he was being slighted, or ridiculed, or patronized off the stage. He hated to be addressed as Little Tich, and anyone guilty of such over-familiarity would be routed with an icy glare and a kingly snub (though he used the name of 'Harry Tich' not only in social and professional relations, but to sign his pictures and sketches). He loathed being stared at and pointed at in the streets: one reason why he had enjoyed living in Paris was that such boorishness was less frequent there than in London. In Budapest, when he was nearly sixty, he found to his delight that nobody in the streets took any notice of his height. In his earlier years especially he seethed with a kind of contained resentment that every now and then broke out in rows with the audience when some of its members displeased him by their behaviour. Harry once said, in later life, that he was quite sure he would have spent most of his life in prison if he had knocked down all the people he *wanted to* knock down for being rude, or condescending, or bullying. He was joking, but he meant it. And there were times when, as Jules Renard noted in his 1903 diary, Tich declared that 'il n'aime pas le comique' and 'deteste le music-hall'.

It was partly because of this nervous susceptibility (combined with sensitivity about his fingers) that Harry was too depressed, at times, to take the stage; and that he sometimes walked off it, in a rage, because he had been insulted—or imagined that he had been insulted, as on the occasion when a man in the stalls continued to read a paper after Tich made his entry. Friends were frequently called in to use their influence on this very shy and very proud little artist. According to Eddie Espinosa in his auto-biography, 'I was very often the means of soothing down his temperamental outbursts and getting him to play when he fully intended to "refuse to go on." ' Yet sometimes there were—as other artists demonstrated—good reasons for walking off. When Tich did this in Sheffield in 1909, because of rowdyism by uni-versity students, the *Performer* commented: 'the better class of the audience appreciated him all the more for his decided action, although they had to share in the punishment'. By refusing to continue working in such conditions Little Tich, and others who did the same, helped to improve the manners of the public and the standards of management.

Naomi Jacob went so far as to say (in *Our Marie*): 'Never was there a man or an artiste who demanded so much deference, so much attention, or who could be, on occasion, so difficult.' Her testimony seems, in some respects, extravagantly loaded: as in her assertion that Tich 'rarely went out in Paris except after dark, and if he had to sally forth in the daytime, hid in the recesses of a cab, cowering as if he was "wanted by the police" '. But it does appear to be true that, as she says, he was 'almost morbidly sensitive', that he 'hated to be noticed and made con-spicuous', and that he was 'inordinately shy about his lack of inches'. Some of his inner feelings are suggested in one of the stories he told reporters, apparently against himself. On his way home from the theatre in Manchester, Tich said, he saw a hawker selling trick paper butterflies.

> I had no coppers, so I gave the man a shilling, declined the butterflies and wished him a good night. He returned me my shilling and said, 'Thanks, I don't take money from boys.'
>
> Somebody then informed him that I happened to be Little Tich, so he chased me and said, 'Mr Tich, I have made a mistake. I *do* take money from boys.'
>
> I said, 'You do?'
>
> He said, 'Yes, sir, I do.'
>
> I said, 'That won't work. Since you left me I have grown up.'

94

Harry Relph had suffered long enough from his abnormality of height, to comprehend the hardships of those who were even more cruelly handicapped, and to defend them against the stupidity, insensitivity and even brutality of the Big People. Among the midgets and dwarfs of show business, in an era when sophisticated audiences still felt no guilt in laughing at the traditionally amusing spectacle of deformity in action, Little Tich became known as a champion; more, a symbol of indestructible cheerfulness—and possible success. The treatment by Big People of the Little People was one of the human phenomena that made him lose his temper. In Blackpool, during the 1920s, he took his mistress and daughter to a circus which featured a Toy Town, peopled by midgets all of whom Harry knew. 'People just don't realize the sufferings of these men and women,' he explained to his little girl. 'Although they may look like children, they are fully grown-up adults with fully adult feelings. Some are extraordinarily clever. Take that man over there'—he pointed at the 'mayor' of Toy Town—'he speaks eight languages, and his sons are all at university, all of normal height, though his wife's a midget.' When Harry introduced his family to the 'mayor' and his fellow-midgets, they treated him as a hero. (It turned out that the 'mayor' had divorced his midget wife and married a woman well over two feet taller than himself). Some years later, on a trip from Australia to England, Little Tich passed the ship's improvised swimming pool to see a crowd of passengers guffawing at some of Lester's Midgets (a well-known stage act of that time) trying to enjoy their bathe in private. He turned angrily on the Big People. 'How would *you* like to be laughed at when you're bathing,' he said, with concentrated fury. 'You seem to forget that these people are men and women, just the same as you. But a good deal more intelligent than *you* are.' The crowd evaporated, and Tich strode on, simmering.

According to Jean Boullet, writing twenty years after his death in the medical journal *Acsculape* (February, 1949), the name of Little Tich was venerated among little people—with those of successful midgets and dwarfs such as Pieral, Jerry Austin and Delphin (the first Tyltyl in *The Blue Bird*)—to a point where it may have saved men and women from suicide (disproportionately frequent among the disproportionately small).

For a man as painfully shy and self-conscious about his height and his hands as was Harry Relph, the processes of courtship—indeed, the very idea of it—must have presented formidable and even frightening problems in his early years. To be laughed at on the stage was a proof of success as an artist. To be ridiculed off the stage was a torment that he continually anticipated and against which he tried to protect himself throughout his life. One of the likeliest ways for a man of four feet six to be ridiculed was to pursue a girl at least six inches taller who did not appear to fancy him. Yet all the women in Harry Relph's life were taller than he was—some almost as tall as those whom he chased, or who chased him, in pantomimes and musical plays. Once he had became a star, he was often wooed and not infrequently won; and several women of his own choice towered above him.

Nothing is known today about Harry's romantic and/or sexual encounters during his teens, from the time he started his professional career in Chatham until he left for America eight years later, at the age of twenty. For a bright, personable, ambitious boy, working his way around provincial towns in the 1880's, it should not have been especially difficult to have picked up an *éducation sentimentale* in the world of music hall. Although Harry was unusually small, he also had exceptional vitality, both mental and physical, and distinctive charm. In spite of his sensitivity about his disabilities it seems probable that by the time he arrived in Chicago he had acquired a sufficiency of sexual experience to give him confidence, having learned that women found him attractive and that among the emotions he inspired in them was the mothering (and, sometimes, smothering) instinct.

Then, in Chicago, he fell head over heels in love. Laurie Brooks was an English girl, a year Harry's junior, in 'The Crystal Slipper'. She was pretty, dark-eyed, dark-haired and petite; perhaps no more than five feet in height. Her home was near one of the worst slums of Victorian London—Lisson Grove, off the Marylebone Road, where Eliza Doolittle came from. At first Laurie was unimpressed by Harry's wooing. There was no instant return of affection: indeed, she tried to discourage him and at first refused his proposals of marriage. But he went on pursuing her, from city to American city, risking one humiliation after another. Laurie may have been influenced by his persistence as well as his charm, and even more, perhaps, by his box-office success. In any event, by the end of the year he had worn down her resistance. On 20 January 1889 Laurie Brooks and Harry Relph were married in Cook County, Illinois.

Within a few weeks Laurie became pregnant. When 'The

Crystal Slipper' ended its run it seems unlikely that she returned with Harry on his short trip to London, or that she rejoined the Chicago company in 'Bluebeard, Junior'. But in September Harry broke away from that show and they sailed for England. The Relphs settled in Lambeth in a house where Harry had stayed on his spring expedition, at 182 Kennington Road, in a district popular with music hall artists. (Chaplin spent part of his childhood nearby.) It was here—on 7 November 1889—that their first child, Paul, was born. Characteristically Harry told this story about the great event—to, among others, Max Beerbohm, a man close to him in height, though Max said, 'I felt gross beside him.'

> When his son was born he was in a state of great anxiety, and he was sitting on the stairs, with his head bowed in his hands and wondering how everything was going, and presently the doctor came along and comforted him. 'It's all right, my little man,' he said. 'You've got a baby brother.'

Not long after Paul's arrival Harry felt that he could splash out on a bigger and more comfortable home, now that he had jumped to the top of the tree. Everything was going right for him, at work and at home. The Relphs' next home was a much more substantial building, in the neighbouring suburb of Clapham: Clifton House, in Clapham Road, close to the homes of such established music hall stars as G. H. Macdermott, and right next door to Dan Leno, who became an intimate friend. Screened from the traffic by tall trees and thick shrubs, with a wide carriage-drive leading to the front door, Clifton House had an orchard, a kitchen garden and a big flower garden, in which Harry spent much of his scanty leisure. The stables held a brougham and a Ralli cart; and above the red-painted coach-house was Harry's den, a studio in which he kept his cello, music, books, photographic equipment, paint boxes and some of his own paintings—largely those of flowers, animals and seascapes. Here, too, were his press cuttings and professional trophies: the gold medal from Tony Pastor; a pair of silver candlesticks from the directors of the Princes in Manchester; a gold cup from the management of Ronacher's. He kept here a portrait of his mother and his big boots.

We know such domestic details because while the Relphs lived in Clifton House Harry was frequently interviewed there, with every appearance of pride and pleasure. He sang the praises of

97

his wife; he showed off the photographs of his little boy ('her very image', he declared); he exuded the happiness of a man who believes he has found the meaning of life. But he was soon to leave his den in the Clapham Road; and for the next thirty years readers of the theatrical and popular press were seldom, if ever, readmitted to any of Little Tich's sanctums, or allowed to find him at home. On the occasions when he did give interviews, it was nearly always in dressing-rooms and bars. His private life was kept strictly private. For that reticence, it appears, there were to be more than usually sufficient reasons.

Harry was soon so much in demand on the Continent that he took a flat in Paris, and about 1894 he left Clifton House and moved there with his family. He found it easier to use this as his base, relying on hotels when he was working in England. The Relphs agreed that Paul should begin school in Paris, which was now their home. But it did not work out quite as they had planned. One day in 1897 Harry returned to the flat from a tour to find that Laurie had disappeared, in fact absconded, 'without a word of warning, not a hint'. What is more, she had stripped the flat bare. She had taken every piece of furniture and every penny of Harry's savings, which, peasant-like, he had kept at home. According to family tradition, they amounted to a small fortune in contemporary terms: £4000 or more. She had gone to Berlin with a lover—a French actor, Francois Marty. And she had left Paul and Harry behind, without a goodbye. She apparently never saw either of them again. Many years later Harry said (to his third wife):

> The thing that upset me most was that she had no heart: she abandoned the boy, you see. It was bad enough to find what she had done, and the manner in which she did it. But to leave the boy behind, that was cruel. I could never forgive her for that.

Laurie's desertion came as a crippling blow to both her husband and her son. We do not know of anything that may have precipitated it on his side, of any excuse for such an abrupt and final betrayal. His absences on tour in England, Germany, Austria and other European countries may well have left Laurie feeling in limbo in the Rue Lafayette flat, alone—except for her son—in the heart of the international capital of fun. Yet the fact that, a

98

few months earlier, he had made a hit in Paris, too, should have compensated for that—if the marriage had been going well, in other respects. Plainly, she must have become bored with Harry as a husband; and he just hadn't noticed, any more than he'd noticed that she had acquired a lover. Perhaps *he* had made *her* jealous: her story was never told. He may already have met the woman who was to be his second wife. But possibly Laurie had never been in love with Harry: a possibility that was, for him, an instant certainty when he found that she had not only deserted him but robbed him, too. Whatever extenuating circumstances there might have been for Laurie's walk-out, it is hard to think of any that might justify her robbery of Harry and her abandonment of Paul.

The paragraphs above contain almost all that we can discover about Laurie Relph, née Brooks. Harry did not talk about her. She remains a mystery. When she made her will, two years after she had deserted Harry, she gave as her temporary address the Paris flat in which they had lived together, although she described herself as 'a married woman living separate and apart from her husband'. Why? Perhaps because for some tactical reason—it was, undoubtedly, a 'good address'—the fiction was a convenient one (Francois Marty lived at the time in the Rue Pigalle). But could she actually have gone back to the old Relph flat to live? And is it possible that Harry didn't *know*, if that were so? In any event, it was soon all over: Laurie Relph died in a Berlin clinic within four years of abandoning her husband and son. Her estate of just under £2900 was divided, after small bequests of £250 each to two male English 'friends' (one of them, mysteriously, had the same name as herself) between Francois Marty (she asked him to bury her in France) and Paul. Her son was to receive £250 when he was twenty-one, and from then until he was thirty he was to enjoy the income from a trust fund set up from his half of the estate. Laurie's brief will, her husband's story of her desertion and a youthful photograph in his private album—this is all that remains of the girl from 'The Crystal Slipper' who broke Little Tich's heart. Her very existence was unknown to most of Harry's friends and relations in later life. Laurie Brooks became a non-person. It was as if she and Harry had never married: except that Paul was there to remind him.

After she left, that terrible day in the Rue Lafayette, not a word seems to have appeared in the press, on either side of the

Channel. Laurie's disappearance was kept a secret even from many of the family, although Harry naturally confided in Agnes and (for strategic reasons) in Millie, his only unmarried sister. One of his decisions, in trying to put the pieces of his life together, was to send Paul to a good English school—in Dulwich. Millie lived nearby in South Norwood, and it was to her care that Harry entrusted his son. He wanted Paul to have the kind of education he had missed; and he believed, no doubt, that this new experience would help to carry his son through the misery of living without his mother. Harry himself could not look after Paul on his own; nor would he return to London to live. Paris was not only more convenient, but much more private. He needed privacy. So he kept his home in Paris, and worked harder than ever before. He had to ensure that his career was not damaged by this personal disaster. Work was what he had to live for. He always put his career first. Harry's secrecy about Laurie's desertion was due not only to his very vulnerable pride but also to a prudent regard for convention. A scandal of that kind could have been damaging to an international celebrity like Little Tich. He could not be seen to fail, he believed, on the stage or in the home. And so the barriers around the boy from Cudham were raised still higher and made still stronger; while behind them the Funniest Fellow on Earth riveted on an extra layer of armour plating.

9

ENTER JULIA

I remember him standing on a little stool and saying, 'That's the height I should like to be.'
                                    Winifred Relph, Little Tich's third wife.

After Laurie left him, Harry was not alone for long. That year (or maybe some months earlier) he had met at the Olympia in Paris a Spanish dancer who had worked in the *corps de ballet* there since the music hall opened in 1890, and had become the second principal dancer. Her name was Julia Amparo Celeste Récio; and she was to live with Harry Relph as his wife for the next twenty-nine years. Their relationship (as seen largely through his own eyes in its last phase) is among the most puzzling of the enigmas in the private life of Little Tich.

Julia Récio was born in Malaga, the daughter of a 'government official', but was brought up in Paris. Her brother Emile ran a menswear shop specializing in shirts and ties close to the Moulin Rouge, with many musicians and performers among his customers. Julia was engaged by her compatriot, the Barcelona-born impresario Joseph Oller, who invented the Pari-mutuel and founded Paris's first racing journal, *Le Bulletin des courses,* in addition to starting the Montagnes Russes, the Moulin Rouge, the Olympia and the Jardin de Paris. There was a persistent vogue for Spanish dancing at this period, and Julia thrived on that. When Julia met Harry at the Olympia she was—like Laurie and like Harry's mother in her youth—dark, petite (four foot eleven) and very pretty; a vivacious, gregarious, extravagant girl, who loved music, animals, birds and children. She said she was eighteen, although Harry claimed to have discovered, many years later, that she was twenty-eight—almost his own age (thirty). Whatever went wrong between them later, at the blackest hour in Harry's life she brought him comfort, affection, excitement and reassurance. She helped to compensate him in private for his humiliation by Laurie, and to cover up in public for Laurie's disappearance. Somehow,

101

in spite of her imperfect English, Julia slipped into the role of Mrs Relph and stayed in it. About 1898, after a press silence of some years about Little Tich's domestic arrangements, 'Mrs Relph' and 'Mrs Tich' reappeared in interviews, yet now she was not English but Spanish.

Two years before Laurie's death Little Tich was telling journalists that he had been married to Julia Récio for nearly three years. He was, in fact, still married to Laurie Brooks. He made these statements without any apparent fear that the real Mrs Relph—or, indeed, any of the people who had known Laurie during her eight-year marriage to Harry—would tell the press the truth. If any questions were then raised publicly about Harry's 'marriage' to Julia and the disappearance of Paul's mother, we have found no trace of them; they made no ripples in the trade press, and cast no shadow on his public reputation under the harsh, bright light that focused on the elite of international show business. How was it that Harry could so confidently declare that he was married to Julia, while his wife was still alive and (as seems likely) back in Paris, back for a time perhaps in their old flat? Did he assume, from his knowledge of Laurie's character, that her sense of guilt about her behaviour would make her stay silent—and keep Francois Marty quiet? Or is it possible (however bizarre it may seem) that Harry *paid* her to keep quiet, in order to make sure that—whatever his private grief and anger—his career could proceed without undue interruption or damaging publicity? Here be more mysteries. What seems clear is that Julia Récio was living with Harry in what the *Era* described, in 1899, as a 'handsome' flat in the Boulevard Poissonière, the street where Julia's brother had his shop; and that—again, to quote the *Era*—Harry had made his home in Paris (though 'the Actor's Bible' made no mention of Julia or of Mrs Relph).

Although Laurie died in 1901, it was not until three years later that Harry Tich married Julia Récio—in London, at the St Giles' Registry Office, on 31 March 1904. This ceremony appears to have been kept successfully secret, no small feat. The apparently complete absence of any press reports is surprising, in view of the conspicuous appearance of so popular a star as Little Tich; but this secrecy was eminently desirable. After all, the bridegroom had been describing the bride as his wife four years earlier, and had told at least one journalist that the wedding had taken place in 1897. In 1904 Harry may, indeed, have been a reluctant groom, as members of his family came to believe. Unwilling to admit that the Relph-Récio affair could ever have been a love match, they suspect that Harry may have been blackmailed into marriage—and staying married. Members of Julia's family, on the other hand (who knew nothing, long after Julia's death, about Laurie) believe that Harry and Julia *were* in love at the start of their relationship, and that its failure was Harry's fault: that, having transplanted her from Paris to London, he consistently neglected her for other women. Harry is reported as saying, later in their marriage, 'I tried for five years to shake her off, but she wouldn't leave me alone. Every time I came to England she'd follow me. I'd send her back to Paris, but she kept returning. A friend of mine said to me one day, "Harry, if you don't do something about that woman, you'll never get rid of her." Well, I never did.' It seems, even now, a somewhat unusual way of talking about one's wife; but it appears to describe the five years before their marriage. And why, if this were so, did Julia persevere so obstinately, refusing to be turned away? Because she loved Harry so deeply; or because her honour was at stake, and he *owed* her marriage; or because (as members of Harry's family believed) she had an eye on the main chance and wanted his money? If, by the time she talked him into marrying her (if that is how it happened) Julia was not twenty-six but *thirty-six,* the need for marriage was all that much more apparent. Be that as it may, both bride and groom gave their address at the wedding in 1904 as a flat off the Tottenham Court Road—44, Bedford Court Mansions—which Harry had rented for the past eighteen months. Two years after the wedding, the Relphs moved to bigger premises in the same block near Bedford Square: to be precise, they took over *two* flats. Their address was Number 79, Bedford Court Mansions; but that was where Harry lived. Although the partition between the flats had been removed, it would be true to say, in marital terms, that Julia lived next door, at Number 78. They maintained that design for living for twenty years, until it was ended by death. And whatever earlier passions may have flowered it seems doubtful that they often—if at all—slept together during those two decades. The marriage foundered rapidly (if it ever got under way), although the alliance continued, indestructibly. They shared a love of music (she played the piano and guitar, he played the cello); chess; billiards; painting; and

103

handing out gifts, with often munificent generosity. According to Naomi Jacob, 'Harry Relph was a most incurable present-giver: what that form of amusement must have cost him every year, I tremble to think.' He also liked, before the First World War, to gamble every now and then. On a six week holiday to Vienna, he told an Austrian interviewer, he had gone to the casino every day and lost all his money; though he won it back later by working at Ronacher's. According to a Manchester reporter in 1908, 'If there is one thing that has impressed him more than another it is the life at Monte Carlo, where he appears regularly. He loves to watch the crowd in the casino, and he is not averse to having a five franc piece on himself. Like most others for whom Monte Carlo has a special attraction, Tich has studied possible winning systems. The subject of Chance may one day be treated by this clever little man; he has known both sides.' Yet, on the other hand, Tich was careful, even meticulous, in his accounting: his daughter has preserved a notebook in which—for the benefit of his tax returns—his annual *professional* income and expenditure was recorded and analyzed, over a decade. He would take a gamble or hand out a generous 'sub' to some old pro down on his luck, yet he was capable of counting the pennies, too, and be seen to count them—not surprising alternations in conduct from a man who had known extremes of poverty and prosperity.

Although Harry and Julia shared little else, from 1906 onwards they shared the two-flat complex in Bedford Court Mansions, which amounted to ten rooms (and a bathroom for each): there were two servants' bedrooms, a large kitchen, a billiard-room, a huge dining-room and drawing-room. On one side of the communal living-space were Harry's bedroom and study; on the other side Julia's bedroom and boudoir. It was filled with heavy French furniture from Paris. During the last part of their life here they were looked after by a housekeeper-cook, a maid (the housekeeper's niece) and a daily char. Harry had a chauffeur (for years this post was filled by Mr Perfect) and—until the 1920's, at least —a valet-dresser. In more prosperous days, it seems, Julia had a car and chauffeur of her own, and two maids.

Throughout most of the twenty years of their co-existence in this double-flat their life-styles were markedly different. Julia was a great party-giver. Harry was not. Publicity paragraphs about him are rare (he never employed a press agent) and his name seldom appears in connection with social functions in the music hall
104

press of the period, which often published detailed lists of the eminent (and not-so-eminent) attending charity dinners; sports meetings; anniversary parties; presentations; dances; special matinees and other events. We have perused scores of these lists: the absence of Tich's name—allowing for his frequent absences from London on tour—indicates unmistakably that even in his earlier years he was (as Don Ross remembers him in his last period) ungregarious and set apart from the off-stage life of his professional colleagues. Leno and Robey were among those he liked and admired, and other friends at different periods in his life included Harry Lauder, R. G. Knowles, Seymour Hicks, Henry Ainley, the painter Jan van Beers, the cellist August van Biene, the boxer Billy Wells, and the novelist Sax Rohmer. But, as his third wife said, Tich 'had little time for those who were not kindred spirits': he made no attempt to sustain the instant, universal bonhomie widely expected from comedians off the stage.

One of his very rare appearances in the gossip columns of a trade paper in 1907 is, characteristically, concerned with Julia: Tich had, says the paragraph, entertained a party of friends to celebrate his wife's birthday. 'The company included, among others, the Marquis de Gandelarias, M. le Comte de Pradere, Professor Arbos, Sênor Alvarez, M. Adrian Vivas, Madame Chavita (from the Opéra Comique, Paris), Senor de la Torre, and Mr and Mrs R. G. Knowles, etc.' Only the last-mentioned couple belong to the British music hall world. It sounds like Julia's party. When Julia entertained—frequently and lavishly—it often caused Harry acute irritation and considerable expense. Julia liked Pomeranians: at one time she had five of them. Harry did not. Julia liked caged birds: she had a cockatoo and thirty canaries. Harry hated them, though he was credited by at least one journalist with their collection. What with the birds, the dogs and the parties, life in Bedford Court Mansions, Harry complained, was Bedlam. The longer Julia was in England, he also complained, the more Spanish she became. When they were on speaking terms, she often spoke to him in Spanish, and he replied in French. French, indeed, was an everyday language in the flat. And yet she would still often come with him on his trips (especially when he went back to Paris in the 1920's), sometimes bringing a selection of her beloved birds, a French maid and a formidable collection of luggage: observed by the press but never interviewed by them, because (so Harry explained) she did not speak fluent English—or would only speak Spanish.

When in London Harry spent an increasing amount of time at his club, the Eccentric. Julia suspected him of spending it in other ways: she always kept the post-box in the flats locked, and had all the mail brought to her first. Her suspicions were sometimes justified. In the course of research for this book it has emerged that Harry had *another* permanent home in London. In 1903—shortly after he took over 48, Bedford Court Mansions— he leased a house in Kilburn (1 Teignmouth Road), which had just been built; and he was a tenant for fifteen years. It seems highly probable that this was not a property speculation—he never showed the smallest interest in letting and sub-letting—but that it was a personal retreat for Harry in which he could get away from Julia and entertain friends in privacy. Significantly, the lease was terminated not long after he met the girl who was to be his third wife, and settled into a new phase of extra-marital fidelity. The fact that he never disclosed to her the existence of this Kilburn house has led their daughter to suggest that it was *Julia* who had kept up the lease, without Harry knowing, as a venue for her own double life. Certainly, among the more surprising aspects of Little Tich's private life is that he could find *time* in it for the house in Teignmouth Road, when he worked outside London for a large part of most peacetime years; and that he did not appear to suspect that Julia might also be having affairs, as their own sexual relationship had ended early in their marriage and they seemed to be emotionally incompatible. Yet there is no doubt that Harry was involved—up to 1916 at least—with a series of 'concubines', as he called them, and one or more of them may have been set up for a while at the house in Kilburn. Harry seems a likelier tenant of 1 Teignmouth Road than Julia, in spite of facts that later emerged about the private life of the second Mrs Relph.

It was not Julia's attitude to sex that worried Harry but her attitude to money. With a conventional male belief in double standard morality he seemed to take it for granted that, whatever his own infidelities may have been, she was faithful to him; or perhaps, in view of his indifference to her and the failure of their marriage, he did not *care* whether she took a lover or not. What *did* concern him, what worried him persistently and intensely, was Julia's extravagance. She liked comfort, indeed luxury, and

106

Harry gave her accordingly a generous allowance. She liked furs, jewellery and fashionable clothes, and Harry paid for these. She liked entertaining, and Harry paid for her parties. She liked to help people, not only emotionally but financially, and Harry subsidized her generosity. Frequently, in later years, he had to pay big bills that she allowed to accumulate. She got into debt, and often had to ask Harry for supplementary cheques because she had mortgaged her allowance. Harry never quite knew, he said, what she did with the thousands he gave her, over the years; but he went on giving. 'I *know* it's serious,' he would say. 'But there's nothing, absolutely nothing, to be done about it.' In the early 1920s, when his income plummeted in one year by nearly two thirds, and, though it rose again, never regained the earning heights of 1907 to 1922, Harry *had* to do something. One of the things he did was to cut Julia's allowance; but, although this caused her deep distress (and is remembered by one of her dependants as some kind of cruel punishment by Harry), it made little difference to her spending. After so many years of unrestricted material comfort she could no longer adapt to economic pressures; and, in any event, she could not reduce the needs—and demands—of her dependants (not all of whom were known to Harry), though they included his own grand-daughter. We shall meet those dependants in later chapters. Meanwhile, we must record that Harry cashed in at least £12,000 of his investments at this period and a £3000 endowment insurance, and that he put the blame on Julia for dissipating his capital in the 1920s—he gave the figure of £20,000.

How did he put up with it? Why didn't he stop the extravagance? Why did he continue the public appearance of a dutiful, contented husband? Why didn't he leave her? At one time or another, there were women ready and willing to live with him, even if Julia wouldn't divorce him.

At Harry's death his son Paul said, 'Father and Julia never loved one another. Poor, poor father. His life was one long misery through her.' So why didn't he *end* the misery? What kept them together?

10

PAUL

As Lupino Lane grew up the two became close friends . . . [Little Tich was twenty-three years his senior, known to him as Uncle Harry.] Sometimes, when there was no matinee, they would take a tram out into the country. On one occasion [in the early 1900's] they came to a wide ditch, which Lupino Lane jumped without difficulty but which proved too much for Little Tich, who finished up to his waist in mud. A kindly farmer allowed him to undress in front of his kitchen fire and even produced the only suit they could find to fit him—a child's sailor suit with hat to match. Far from being embarrassed, Little Tich was delighted . . . On the tram back to London he pretended to be Lupino Lane's little brother, insisted on sitting on his lap and generally managed to act the naughty boy. He knocked a man's hat off, tripped the conductor, and cheeked a fat lady on the next seat. 'I'd tan his hide if he was mine,' said the fat lady to the embarrassed Lupino Lane. Eventually she took matters into her own hands and gave Little Tich a hearty cuff. 'That's what comes of being too funny,' said Tich ruefully as he rubbed his ear.

James Dillon White, *Born to Star*, 1957.

As Little Tich's only son, Paul Relph merits a place in this shadowy group portrait, although his character and his later life rank among the many mysteries of the story.

As we have seen, Paul was born to Laurie and Harry Relph in November 1889 at their first London home, 182 Kennington Road. After an infancy spent in the bigger house in Clapham, Paul moved with his parents to Paris and went to school there. Paul seemed in his childhood to be gifted with many advantages: he was a handsome and intelligent boy, with his mother's dark eyes, black hair and sharp features, and something of his father's physical agility, dancing talent and artistic sensibility—but none of his physical disabilities (his adult height was nearly five foot eight). His father doted on him. There seemed to be love and money to spare.

108

Then, when he was seven, Paul's mother suddenly disappeared; he was hurried off to a new school in London; and he was put in charge of his Aunt Millie, Harry's unmarried sister. Aunt Millie was a severe, joyless spinster, remembered by her family as a virago. Whatever her virtues, she seems to have been altogether unfitted to look after a small, bewildered, miserable boy who had, in effect, lost both his parents at a stroke. In the space of a few months his mother had left him and his father had sent him away, a combination of disasters likely to damage the psyche of the most secure and sturdy child. As he grew older and began to tower above his father, Harry's height became an additional complication.

For the next seven years, from seven to fourteen, Paul seldom saw his famous father. At some time during this period he was taken from his London school to one in Paris, but this made little difference to his relationship with Harry. Harry would visit 'Boy', as he called him, as often as he could whenever he was in London. Paul would stay with them on his holidays, if Harry and Julia were not touring, and sometimes travel with them to Berlin, Vienna, Madrid and other dates. He understood, on a conscious level, why Harry was so often away or unavailable. He understood, increasingly, the suffering his mother had caused his father. He was proud of Harry, and he liked his stepmother: in childhood, at least, they got on well—she was at her best with children. But the early damage was, it seems, irreparable, and it showed: first of all, and most conspicuously, in a stammer. Paul's was a bad stammer; it was never cured; and it got worse as he grew older. In his twenties it developed into a choking affliction that remained for the rest of his life, exaggerated by wartime shell shock. Conversation with Paul Relph was sometimes an ordeal, both for Paul and for anyone to whom he was talking. It appears to have been a painful symbol of a larger failure in communication.

Another symptom of Paul's problems was his relative failure at school, in spite of his natural intelligence. He found it almost impossible to 'get on' as well as his father expected; and, as is the way of fathers, Harry expected all the more because his own education had stopped so abruptly and so early. For this and other reasons Paul found it harder to get on with Harry, in spite of his affection and admiration for his father. Long before his childhood dragon, Aunt Millie, died in 1909, Paul had suffered

109

that familiar sea-change from being a 'sweet little boy' into 'a great disappointment'.

Paul Relph didn't go to a university. He didn't get into the City. He didn't go into any of the professions. He didn't take up the watchmaking trade in which Harry had him trained. He didn't become a businessman. He didn't do anything that his father had hoped for. That, in itself, is no more unusual than either growing or aging pains; and among the traditional manifestations of the latter discomforts is a profound disillusionment with filial careers and life-styles. What Paul did do was to follow his father into the world of show business. It was the one thing he was determined to do, whatever anyone might say, and in spite of that crippling stammer. Perhaps, in part, it was *because* of the stammer that Paul set his heart on being a performer. On the stage, he felt, he could liberate himself—as his father had done—from the embarrassments and humiliations of his disability, expressing himself in song and dance. Moreover, he had seen at first hand, both in Britain and on the Continent, the heady psychological bonuses, as well as the glittering financial rewards, that success in variety theatres could bring. His insistence on following that career seems, in retrospect, little more surprising than his overestimation of his own talent or his emotional ambivalence with regard to his father. What is harder to understand is Harry's attitude to Paul; but that is, no doubt, because the details of Paul's behaviour to his father are among the mysteries of Little Tich's career.

Harry didn't want Paul to go into show business. He thought Paul was unsuited to the stage: partly because of the stammer—so Harry told him—he didn't have the makings of a comic. Harry wanted Paul, at one time, to go into business. Then, as he told Max Beerbohm, he wanted him to take holy orders. He was 'dreadfully worried' about Paul before World War I, Beerbohm said (as reported by S. N. Behrman).

I met him one night in a pub near Her Majesty's and found the dear man in a state of particular depression. 'Oh,' he said. 'My boy! I don't know what will become of him. He is not serious. He is not religious. I'm afraid he hasn't a vocation. Instead of studying he prefers to hang around your brother's theatre. He's probably in there right this minute. If he can't get a seat, he stands at the back of the stalls.'

110

t 21: on the threshold of fame

Agnes Relph, Harry's favourite
sister, at 23-24, in 1886

Harry's first wife, Laurie Brooks,
at 22, a year after their marriage

Paul Relph and his
stepmother Julia

Paul Relph and his
daughter Constance

Julia Relph, Rudy Knoepper (her adopted son) and Frederic Recio (her nephew), 1917

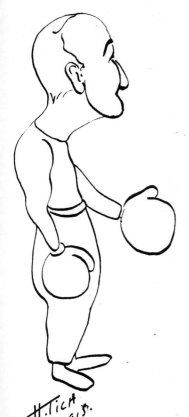

The Pugilist: a caricature by Tich of himself, 1915

Little Tich in the 1890s
playing the cello, his
favourite instrument for
half a century

At home in Clapham, c.1891

Sinbad the Sailor, 1916: 'from
nbad to Hinbad' (Ivey Latimer,
later the third Mrs Relph)

As an 'officier d'Académie',
wearing his much-prized honour
from the French Goverment, of
the *palmes académiques*

Alfred Bryan cartoon from
Entr'acte, 1896

TLE *TOMNODDY TICH, TO MR. BEERBOHM TREE*:—"I AM LOOKING
FOR A LONDON HOUSE, AND WILL TAKE THE HAYMARKET OFF
YOUR HANDS, IF YOU LIKE!"

Ivey Latimer, later the third
Mrs Relph ('Win')

Harry at 55

Thumbnail sketch made by Little Tich
for his daughter, Mary

Golfing with Harry Lauder,
1913, from 'The Tatler'

With a Paris gendarme in the 1920s

Harry, Win and their daughter Mary in the Royal Botanic
Gardens, 1924

The last photograph of Little Tich,
at 60, taken on stage, in 1927, at
the London Palladium

With Mary, on board ship, in 19

Whatever agonies Harry endured on Paul's behalf it does seem from our vantage point that for all his compassionate understanding and paternal affection Harry underestimated the impact on his son of Laurie's desertion, Millie's pseudo-motherhood, his own absences, the burden of the stammer and the effect of his fame, as both goad and paralyzer. Harry knew that Paul had gone through a bad time, but he probably did not realize quite *how* bad; and he was inclined—again, like most fathers—to tell himself (and, no doubt, to tell Paul too) that it only needed a bit of effort, hard labour and concentration to succeed, as he himself had succeeded, against much heavier odds than Paul had been obliged to contend with. Harry had done so, moreover, without the benefit of a good education and a wealthy father's backing.

When Harry finally acquiesced in Paul's decision to be an entertainer at all costs, he gave his son, from the wisdom of his experience, some fatherly advice. Paul might, he said, do very well at dancing, if he would really work hard at it. In view of his vocal disability he would do well to concentrate on that. But, whatever he did, he should make it his very own. 'Above all things, be yourself. Be an original,' said Harry. 'You'll never be any good if you're not an original. Never copy.' The advice was loving and shrewd; it was also cruel. To very few performers is it given to be 'an original'. It was not given to Paul Relph.

After dropping out of the watchmaking trade he worked with one of Fred Karno's companies. At some time between 1906 and 1910 he appeared in the historic 'Mumming Birds' sketch, about a 'swell' on a night out in a music hall, which Karno kept in profitable circulation for at least thirty-five years. The Karno companies served as the jumping off point for a number of performers who were later to achieve celebrity, notably Charlie Chaplin, with whom Paul worked briefly in 'Mumming Birds'. Paul was not among them. His career is plunged in obscurity. He became a circus clown, where his stammer mattered not at all, reappearing from time to time in music hall, revue and pantomime at the lower end of the scale. And, in default of an original talent, he fell back at one period on his father's act. Long after Harry's death he attempted to cash in on the family name. Calling himself Paul Tich, he used as his selling tag 'Son of a Famous Father—Dancing in Big Boots.' But, even though the big boots were smaller and lighter than Harry's he didn't, it seems, dance well enough—or do anything else well enough. In spite of his charm,

E

intelligence, likeability and a consuming passion for the stage, he wasn't a good enough artist in any line to make a mark. Invoking his father's reputation was more of a hindrance than a help, as many other 'sons of famous fathers' have discovered.

Paul was no more successful in his private life, by conventional standards. He was married at twenty-one in Manchester to a music hall artist, Gilda Nicholas, four years his senior. The following year they had a daughter, Constance Julia: it is significant that Paul included his stepmother's name, an indication that she was then ranked as an ally rather than an enemy, although, according to Relph family tradition, they did not get on well later on. About four years later he abandoned his wife and child, without attempting to make any provision for them. Perhaps there were some mitigating circumstances for leaving Gilda. According to the Relph family tradition, 'there was no happiness in the home for Paul'. But it seems evident that happiness in the home was one thing that Paul Relph did not seek. Gilda took him back more than once in their brief but stormy married life, after he had run off with another woman, but she realized that there was no future to their relationship. Paul's desertion of his child is hard to excuse: especially as he repeated this pattern of behaviour at least once after his marriage broke up, fathering an illegitimate child and walking abruptly away from any paternal responsibilities. In the light of his own broken home and his mother's walk-out it may be easier to understand his conduct, but not to exonerate it.

In the case of Constance, it was Julia who came to the rescue. The little girl had been sent to a convent in Sidcup, Kent, at the age of three, pending the hoped-for reconciliation of her parents. When this failed to materialize, and when Gilda failed to show any eagerness to look after her child, Julia became, in effect, Constance's mother by proxy. Gilda and Paul did not get divorced: Harry did not want them to take this step, because of the scandal it might cause. By way of compensation, to prevent Gilda from suing for a divorce, he settled £1000 on her, the annual interest on this sum passing in due course to Constance. To encourage Gilda to see her daughter, Julia used to send her the train fare to London twice a year. In later years Constance and her mother came closer together, but Gilda died in 1954, at the age of sixty-nine, without ever having remarried. She had not seen her husband for some forty years.

112

Paul Relph continued to visit his father at Bedford Court Mansions every now and then, or in his dressing-rooms: he wanted money, on most occasions. He served in the First World War, was shell-shocked, discharged, and—with the worsening of his stutter—found it increasingly hard to get work. Finally, Harry stopped the handouts. He told Paul that he never wanted to see him again. For Harry Relph, as the years went by, there was nothing to be said for his only son. He would hear no argument in Paul's defence. Paul was dismissed as 'a blackguard and a wastrel'.

I helped him a great deal. He had anything he wanted. But he was no good. He threw away every opportunity put in his way. I even had him trained as a watch-maker, so that he should never be without a living of some sort. Not that he needed to work. Apart from myself, his mother left him well-provided for; but he ran through the lot in a couple of years. He was extravagant and ungrateful. He just couldn't stick at anything. but he wouldn't listen to me. He would go his own way. Women became part of his trouble—all of them the wrong sort. Finally I washed my hands of him. I finished with him completely. Now I never wish to set eyes on him again.

This break between father and son happened when Paul was about twenty-six. They were still unreconciled when Harry died twelve years later.

The trouble was that having spent his own money, and exhausted his credit with his father, Julia, their family and their friends, Paul refused to attempt any kind of employment outside show business. 'Work at something else? *Me?* Unthinkable! The stage is my life,' he would say. 'I wouldn't *dream* of giving it up.' So, while he waited to be recognized, he had no compunction in being subsidized by women, a greater sin in the social calendar sixty years ago than it is today. Whereas his father had pulled himself upwards out of a working class background, Paul turned away from middle class designs for living to the lower reaches of city life, sometimes existing barely above starvation level until a circus or a music hall gave him a job again or another woman—won by his charm and talent for friendship—paid his way.

For the last decade of his life Little Tich did not want to hear about his son, let alone see him. According to his third wife, this was almost the only subject about which he would get very angry, when she pleaded on his son's behalf. 'You know nothing whatsoever about it,' Harry would say. As far as he was concerned, he *had* no son. He tried to dismiss Paul from his mind as finally as he had once dismissed Paul's mother. Long after her death, it seemed to him, Laurie was still punishing him through their son. *Her* son. That, perhaps, was at the root of their trouble.

There were, however, other children in the Relphs' household during much of their married life. Julia was not only stepmother to Paul, but also, as we have seen, a devoted mother to his daughter Constance, who made her home in the Bedford Court Mansions flat from 1914 until Julia's death in 1926 when she was fifteen ('that shattered my life'). Constance was a weekly boarder in a convent at Golders Green (Julia paid the fees), but spent her weekends and holidays with her grandfather and grandmother, who took her with them to Paris on more than one trip. Constance saw her father, if at all, only when he called on Harry to ask for money; and she saw her mother only when Julia sent Gilda the fare to visit Constance in London. It was on Constance's account, it seems, that Julia maintained the big aviary of canaries. The cockatoo was hers. Julia let it be known—among some of Constance's fellow-pupils at the convent, for instance (see chapter 13)—that the girl was not her granddaughter but her daughter by Harry: a family fantasy of which Constance was unconscious and that Harry did nothing to check, if indeed he knew anything about it. Half a century later Constance, who adored her grandmother, remembered her grandfather as a remote and somewhat disapproving presence, although her recollections were no doubt inevitably coloured by her bitterness at what she saw as his ill-treatment of Julia and his later lack of concern about her own future. Harry himself saw relatively little of the child. He was disappointed that she was so obviously a partisan of Julia in that divided household, and that she showed—as it seemed to him—such scant recognition of the fact that it was he who had paid for her upbringing and education. At the same time he felt, one suspects, a continuing resentment that he should have to shoulder the responsibilities of his feckless and ungrateful son, with so little thanks for it.

Yet another virtual foster-child in that crowded Bloomsbury flat, during the greater part of the Relphs' married life, was the younger Julia Récio, daughter of Mrs Relph's brother, Emile. His wife died when Julia was only two, in 1910, and his sister—the elder Julia—took the little girl back with her to London, where she frequently stayed for up to half a year at a time until Julia Relph's death sixteen years later. After half a century she remembered this as the happiest time of her life. To Constance she was, in effect, an elder sister. To Julia Relph they were like her daughters. She expected Harry to pay for them, as if they *were* her daughters; and he did.

There was, however, yet another adopted child in the Relph menage, about whom another of the family mysteries revolves. Rodolphe Knoepper, orphaned in infancy, was the nephew of Harry Alaska, a Russian-born ex-acrobat who was for some years Little Tich's valet and dresser. When Mrs Alaska died, Harry Alaska could no longer look after Roudy—and Julia volunteered to take him over because she was a great friend of his mother. Roudy (born in 1899) was brought up by the Relphs as their son, was educated at Harry's expense in France (both his parents were said to be French) and in London, and came to stay in Bedford Court Mansions on his holidays. Harry liked Roudy, who, he said, treated him better than his own son did; but it was Julia who insisted that the boy lived with them, whenever this was possible. She 'doted' on Roudy. He was *her* adopted son, rather than Harry's. In the First World War Roudy went into the French Army as soon as he was old enough. A family photograph survives in which Roudy stands in uniform with Julia's arm around him, while Paul stands to the side, detached, in civvies. When Roudy was killed in April 1918, Julia is said to have gone almost out of her mind with grief. The intensity of her attachment may be explained by the fact that she could not have children herself. Roudy was, perhaps, a surrogate son, a role in which she could not quite bring herself to accept Paul. Yet it was suspected in Harry's family that it was only by Harry that Julia 'could not have children'; and that Roudy Knoepper was really her own son. The suspicion must be recorded here as an index of inter-family feeling, although we have found no evidence at all to support it. Harry left no word to indicate that he shared it, and it is firmly denied by Julia's surviving relations.

Julia's maternal passion—seeking outlets in other people's children—was clearly deep and unappeasable; perhaps it was this, in part, which had first drawn her to Harry. By contrast, although Harry paid the bills for all these dependants and behaved

115

towards them (as the younger Julia remembers) with kindness and generosity, he was a much more introspective and reserved personality. If Julia and he had shared a child of their own, the story of their marriage might well have been different.

A frequent visitor to this strange and cosmopolitan household, who ranked for many years almost as a member of the family, was a French singer and dancer, Emile Footgers. His real name was Fougerès, which he may well have altered to make it sound more like that of the great clown Footit: a kind of assonance widely practised in show business, as Tich saw to his annoyance in such now obscure imitators as 'Little Pich' and 'Little Rich'. Emile's professional specialities included dancing with a doll his own size, singing scraps of opera in a kind of Franco-Italian vocal potpourri, and singing Anglo-American 'coon' songs with 'a French accent you could ride to York and back on', as he was described in 1904, when singing at the Folies-Bergère. Harry first met him in Paris around that time, and he became one of Harry's few close male friends, often travelling with him in pre-1914 years on his Continental trips when Julia did not come (and sometimes when she did). The Relph family still has a birthday present apparently given by him to Harry in 1909; a solid silver figure of Tich in his Big Boots costume mounted on blue velvet and framed in silver. At one period, when he had apparently settled in London, Emile used to lunch daily at the Relphs' flat: a place was regularly laid for him. In Harry's absences, he was a kind of uncle to the youngsters in the flat. He would take Julia out to dinner and the theatre, from time to time, at Harry's request. Visiting Relphs noted Emile's ubiquity with some alarm; but if they did say anything to Harry, he dismissed their suspicions with the defensive hauteur that repelled any personal intrusions. 'I am very, very fond of Emile,' he would say. And so he remained for many years, until the truth emerged . . .

116

11

THE LAST ROMANCE

I know I earn more than a Prime Minister, but after all I do so much less harm, don't I?
        Little Tich, quoted by Naomi Jacob in *Our Marie*, 1952

By the time that Harry Relph was nearing fifty, in the middle of the First World War, he was still working hard, still at the summit of his profession and still earning a great deal of money—nearly £10,000 a year—in 1915/16, on which he paid over £1500 in income tax and super tax. A great deal of this, it seems, was spent by Julia. Harry also gave generously to family, friends and many good causes including, of course, war charities. He took his pleasures in golf and billiards, playing the cello and sometimes the saxophone, drawing and painting. He didn't drink or smoke very much compared with earlier times. Back in his American days, after living it up with the 'Crystal Slipper' company on tour across the States in prolonged sessions of drinking and card-playing, he had been told by a doctor that both cigarettes and whisky were dangerous for him. He came to respect this warning, although he always liked a drink and continued to take cigars, wine and brandy in moderation. By 1915 Harry rarely went out to parties any more (this abstinence had started before the war) and he seldom entertained at the flat: partly because Julia did so much entertaining on her own account, partly because so many of his professional friends were heavy drinkers, mainly because he had so little time. Harry's evenings were (Sundays excepted) committed to Little Tich for most weeks in most years: he *had* to be on stage. When he came off it, he was seldom in the mood for social events. He was defensive about his height, his hands and his wife. It is perhaps not surprising that he earned the reputation, in some quarters, of being both miserly and misanthropic; but neither slander was based on fact. Harry was a shrewd business man, in his way; he was determined to get his due, financially; and his own

117

tastes were frugal. But he usually spent generously, as far as we can see; and although his range of 'real' male friends was very narrow—in this, as in everything else, he was a perfectionist—within that circle he showed a capacity for warm and open-hearted affection.

As for women, Harry earned something of a reputation as a Don Juan, although he was understandably wary after his experience with Laurie, Julia and several others who cared, he believed, only about his money and his influence. 'Something about him—his brilliant wit, or his quietly authoritative personality—caused women not to see him as a quaint figure of fun, but actually to fall in love with him. His retinue of girl friends looked like a line-up for an international beauty contest,' wrote the wife of 'Sax Rohmer' (Arthur Henry Ward), who ghosted the 'autobiography' that Tich published in 1911, and was a close friend of the comedian for some years. During one affair in his forties he bought the girl a piano, as a proof of his affection, only to learn the following week that she had just got married (and was keeping the piano, thanks very much): she had been engaged to another man all the time. The unrequited feeling was by no means always on his side only. Cautious as he was, Harry was sometimes the pursued rather than the pursuer. Among his more ardent admirers was Jos Collins, who shortly afterwards made her name as the leading lady of 'The Maid of the Mountains'. Miss Collins used to ring Harry up in the middle of the night, demonstrate her personal interest in a number of other embarrassing ways, and, when he finally called on her in order to break off their relationship, she knocked him to the ground. She was, in addition to being angry, considerably taller than Tich. Just as he was moderate in his drinking and smoking, so Harry avoided sexual binges. Yet women continued to be attracted not only by his money and his fame but also by his wit, his vitality, and his gentlemanly behaviour. For some women his height was a special point in his favour, for reasons which one may safely do no more than guess at. But Harry himself was self-disciplined and, one suspects, fairly abstemious in sexual matters. His work always came first; and he needed to concentrate all his energies on keeping Little Tich at the summit. He never had intercourse before a performance. In later life he ceased to be involved in ephemeral affairs and sexual scalp-collecting. Behind his reserve, the especial hauteur of a very small man, Harry craved—like many men in

118

their mid-forties—for the Real Thing: companionship, honest affection, 'true' love from a woman who was understanding yet unsophisticated, good and gentle. Unlike most men in their mid-forties, he found her. Her name was Winifred Emma Latimer Ivey: known on the stage as Ivey Latimer, but known to Harry Relph as Win.

Win was born in Hove, Sussex on 26 February 1892, the youngest of three children. Her mother Harriet Latimer was born in Wolverhampton; and her father James Ivey, born in Brighton, was a commercial traveller in groceries. They had first met as members of the choir and Sunday School teachers attached to a local Congregational church. There were family links with the theatre on Mrs Ivey's side (with the actress Edith Latimer and the actor-author-director Harley Granville Barker), but Win's parents took no interest in the stage—not even in their youngest daughter's later career. She was, in a sense, the Cinderella of the family. She always remembered her mother telling her that she was 'an incident in their lives, of no particular interest'. Like Harry, she lived as a child inside herself, on her own. At the age of fourteen she was taken from her Brighton school and sent to Pitman's to learn shorthand-typing and typewriting, so that she could assist her business-minded brother. Win took it hard that both he and her elder sister had been allowed to stay on at school for much longer before being expected to earn their livings. Although she did help her brother during her two and a half years of Pitman's training (rewarded by an occasional half-crown), she found work elsewhere when the course was over, joining the Brighton Post Office as its first female shorthand typist and secretary to the postmaster. Meanwhile, she continued with the singing lessons, as a promising mezzo-soprano who became—under the tuition of her local teacher, Arthur Whalen—a promising dramatic soprano. Win had paid for her lessons with her own savings and pocket money since she left school: she had received no encouragement from her family, although she was allowed to practise on the piano at home.

At the age of nineteen, Win decided to give up the Post Office and take up singing as her rightful career. She had no job to go to, but started to practise all day and every day, as she had been longing to do. When her money ran out—she found that she owed £2 for a skirt—she applied for an engagement to the owner of a local cinema, the Court, under the name of Ivey Latimer. The proprietor, Mrs Barrasford—widow of Tom Barrasford—booked her for a trial week at £5, to sing in between the silent shorts. Win went down well with the Court customers and Mrs Barrasford, who booked her for another week. She could now pay the bill for her skirt: but something more significant happened. Mrs Barrasford asked her to sing at a charity matinee, which included Gladys Cooper and Seymour Hicks in a sketch they were playing at the Brighton Hippodrome. After the matinee was over, the Hippodrome manager congratulated Win and said he wanted her to appear at his theatre. Seymour Hicks went even further, saying he would get his agent to book her for London. Within a mere two weeks of striking out on her own, Win's courage was remarkably justified.

Hicks was true to his promise. But when his agent contacted Win with an offer to play the juvenile lead in a forthcoming London production, after a tour opening in Manchester, she turned it down. With no encouragement at home, never having travelled anywhere before on her own, the prospect frightened her too much. Immediately afterwards, however, Win received another offer, and—having discovered more precisely what it entailed— signed a three year contract with the big provincial chain of Moss & Stoll for £12 a week, with all touring expenses paid. After appearing at leading music halls throughout the country she arrived in London within four months, making her debut at the Victoria Palace in April 1913, scoring with 'My hero' and 'In the garden of my heart'. Before her contract had expired she had played the Alhambra and the Palace; played the title role in tours *The Merry Widow, Miss Hook of Holland* and *Gypsy Love*: appeared in panto first as Fairy Queen, then Principal Girl and Principal Boy—a familiar ladder of success. Win's family were not impressed: not even by one of the proudest moments of her career when, within a few weeks of embarking on her first tour, she was invited to sing before King George V at Lord Derby's seat, Knowsley Hall, near Liverpool in a Royal Command Performance. She had already given a private performance there before Lord Derby, who presented her with a souvenir in the shape of a gold necklet set with aquamarines and pearls in pendant form. After she had sung before the King, Win was given a gold note-book and pencil in miniature. We mention them here because they were among her most treasured possessions;

120

and her unaffected pride in them was typical of her enthusiastic and somewhat naïve attitude to life, an innocence that, for Harry, was one of her main attractions.

By 1915, when Win first met Harry Relph, she was twenty-three; she was earning £30 a week; and, though beautiful, she had no boy friends. She was totally immersed in her work. She was also totally unawakened physically, a virgin with not even a romantic idyll in her past. She had been engaged as Principal Boy (Hinbad) at the Royal Court Theatre, Liverpool for its 1915 panto, *Sinbad the Sailor*. Sinbad, the starring role, was played by Little Tich. And this is how it began, in the words of the Principal Boy. Win remembered it all very clearly, and often talked of it in later years. There was one other unusual thing about that Christmas: her parents had come to see her on the stage for the first time in five years, at her expense, and she had got her sister, Liz (later Nina), a job in the chorus. It was to be a family Christmas—with, as it turned out, a difference. Win said:

'During a break from rehearsals, four female principals, including myself, went over to the Adelphi Hotel one afternoon for tea in the lounge. While we were awaiting service Mr Tich came in and spotted us. He smiled, crossed over to our table and asked permission to join us. Several weeks later he told me that he had first become attracted to me while chatting over the tea-cups that afternoon. I had been quite unaware of this at the time.'

'I didn't meet him again, off the stage, until Christmas Day. We were all free until 6.30, when final touchings up to the production had to be done. As I came up to the stage door I saw Mr Tich standing under a street lamp, reading what appeared to be a letter. We exchanged greetings and I asked him if he had enjoyed a trip to London he'd told us he was going to make.'

' "I didn't go," he said. "Having spent some time with the boys in the Victoria, I decided not to travel. So I went to bed, and stayed there all day. There was nothing to do, and nowhere to go." '

'I felt very sorry about this, and said so. It seemed incredible that such a famous person should be at a loss for friends and lonely on Christmas Day. So I blurted out that if we had been aware of this, my family and I would have been most happy to have had him join us. To my surprise, Mr Tich replied that if he'd known that, he would most certainly have accepted. On the spur of the moment I suggested that he could still join us in a

121

family party that night for dinner, after the rehearsal. He looked really delighted and said that he would certainly come.'

'That evening was a great success. Mr Tich was a charming guest, and we all liked him. Before leaving us he made an appointment for Liz and me to have lunch with him at the Adelphi, the day after the show opened. When we arrived at his hotel suite, we found him pacing up and down, looking extremely worried and clutching a sheaf of papers. He immediately apologized, but explained that he had just had a shock on opening his post. It included a packet containing bills of huge amounts, extending over three years, about which he had known absolutely nothing. We did our best to overcome the embarrassment of finding him at that moment, and although the atmosphere at lunch in the hotel restaurant was rather subdued at first Mr Tich soon regained his spirits and all was well. Formalities were now dropped. It was "Win" and "Harry" after that.'

From that moment Hinbad was besieged with invitations from Sinbad. He asked her to luncheon, he asked her to tea, he asked if he could escort her back to her hotel after the pantomime was over. He rang her to wish her good morning. His escort-duty became a regular nightly occurrence. When they got to Win's hotel they would sit in the hall, in front of a big open fire, talking to each other while the night porter swept up and cleared up around them, till the fire burned right out and it was too cold to put off saying goodnight any longer. 'This period lives as a vivid picture in my memory,' said Win, years later, 'because during those quiet midnight hours we came to understand each other: confiding our experiences and drawing closer to each other, although love-making played no part at this stage.'

Harry told her everything, or so it seemed. He told her about his boyhood, his hobbies, his work. He told her about Laurie, blaming himself for the failure of the marriage because he had talked her into it. He told her about the miseries of his life with Julia; his anxieties over his son; his financial worries, selling stock to meet Julia's bills. He told her about his 'concubines,' as he called them—including the most recent one for whom he'd bought the piano.

Sinbad the Sailor was a big success. Not only did Little Tich once again score a great personal hit—as was, indeed, expected of the star from London—but Ivey Latimer was widely praised for her performance of Hinbad: notably, for the way she sang

122

the hit of the day, 'Keep the Home Fires Burning', against patriotic tableaux showing a Tommy in the trenches, then back home with his old parents. (Ivor Novello's evergreen song was still so new that reviews also described it as 'Till the Boys Come Home' and 'There's a Silver Lining'.) Miss Latimer was acclaimed for her 'quiet charm and vocal sweetness'; 'breezy without being bold, she is likely to prove exceedingly popular.' She was 'an excellent Principal Boy'. It was to be the pinnacle of her career.

'As the weeks rolled by,' Win recalled, 'Harry and I seemed to become aware that we had fallen in love. One cannot explain how; and I don't recollect it actually being put into words. But time seemed to pass so quickly when we were together. We talked every morning on the phone. Sprays of violets and lily of the valley were almost daily gifts from him. And our senses of humour seemed to coincide.' On her birthday in February he surprised her after luncheon by introducing her in his sitting-room to a jeweller, who had brought a tray of rings with him. Harry picked a solitaire and put it on the fourth finger of Win's right hand.

Although Sinbad and Hinbad had not yet made any formal declaration to each other, it was obvious to most people around that they were very much in love. Word must have reached Julia in London, because one evening during the show Harry suddenly saw her in a box. She had not told him she was coming north to see the pantomime (it was a rare thing for her to do by this time in their lives). She did not come round to see him afterwards. She never mentioned at any time to Harry (so he said) that she had actually seen him in *Sinbad the Sailor*. And she never said anything then or later, Harry declared, about any gossip she may—indeed, *must*—have heard. As long as her role as Mrs Relph was not jeopardized, and she could go on living in her accustomed style, he believed, she was unconcerned (though her adopted daughters testify otherwise at a later date).

On the last night of the pantomime, Hinbad and Sinbad sat up for the last time in front of the open fire in the hall of Win's hotel. Next day Harry was going back to London—and Julia. Win was staying on in Liverpool to do a week at the Empire as a single turn. The moment had come, as Harry knew, for decisions —or, at any rate, for proposals.

'Harry told me that he loved me, and that he needed me in his

123

life; and that during the time we had spent together he had come to the conclusion that I felt the same way about him. I answered, "Yes, I do." Then he said, "Would you consider us becoming lovers? Don't answer now. Take time to consider. Because I can never marry you. My wife is a Catholic. But my feelings will not change and I shall always be true to you." '

'Four proposals of marriage had been made to me since I went on the stage. But I can truthfully say that Harry's request was the first of its kind.'

Win did not give Harry an answer then and there. They agreed to write to each other every day, and to meet shortly in London. When they did meet, it was in Harry's dressing-room at a music-hall in Kingston. 'He was happy with the answer I gave him then,' said Win. Some weeks later, after Harry had accomplished an Irish tour (narrowly missing the Easter Rising) they slept together for the first time—'a precious, snatched, one-night occasion,' as Win described it, at Stoke-on-Trent. 'In giving myself to his needs, it made life easier for Harry; and the fulfilment deepened our affection and trust in one another.' So began the love of both their lives. It mattered not a damn that Win was a foot taller than Harry.

12

LIVING WITH WIN

A comedian who wishes to succeed has a difficult task, especially in music halls where he has to furnish his own material, and work very hard, particularly if, like myself, he works single-handed. I pride myself on being one of the last of the 'old gang' to depend upon his own personal efforts for a livelihood. Most of the others are either with revues or are working in sketches.

Little Tich, 1920.

Although open sexual liaisons were not, of course, unknown sixty years ago, especially in the world of the theatre and wartime London, they were still relatively rare—especially among the famous. Engaged couples did not gossip to columnists about their experiments in bed before marriage. Unhappily married middle class people—especially those who had failed to ascertain their sexual incompatibility in advance—were inclined to observe the conventions and conduct their affairs with traditional discretion, often in mutual collusion. Particular discretion was expected of— or was, at least, advisable in—public idols. Although you could get away with a great deal in show business, it was not thought wise to be seen getting away with it too obviously and too often. One could never be sure if a sudden attack of morality, whipped up by some sanctimonious cleric or sensation-selling journalist, would turn indulgent fans into Puritan witch-hunters.

In any event, no waves of sexual liberation and winds of social change—blowing hard as they were in the war and its aftermath—affected the course of Harry Relph's behaviour. For the next ten years after Winifred Ivey and he first made love together he continued to share a home with Julia; and the woman whom he told he really loved had to maintain a secret life that he could only share with her spasmodically and almost furtively. It was a life of acute and persistent frustration, of inevitable make-believe and deception, of many risks and anxieties—especially for Win.

She seized any opportunities to help Harry in ways that Julia

125

apparently neglected. During the run of the Liverpool panto, for instance, she noticed that—in spite of a very icy spell of weather—Harry did not wear outdoor gloves, because it was difficult to find ones that fitted his hands. After searching the city shops she discovered one which displayed a 'beautifully soft (mohair or cashmere) pair of mittens intended for officers' use. I turned them into bag-like gloves by stitching the open ends of each top together. Harry was delighted and wore them continually.' Later, in London, she tried to find how she could order 'casts' made for hands individually different from the normal range. At a surgical instrument-makers she was told that their resident 'sculptor' of such casts had disappeared with the outbreak of war, but they advised her to contact the manager of Penberthy's in Oxford Street, because it was the only firm in London willing to supply a single glove for members of the Forces who had suffered amputation in the war. When Win met the Penberthy's manager, he suggested that, if her friend called, he would personally make a drawing of each hand and get the gloves made; but when she explained that the friend was Little Tich, the manager agreed to visit Harry in his dressing-room. As a result, in due course, Harry received a dozen pairs of perfectly fitting gloves, made in antelope, suede and kid, which he wore continually—as occasion required—during the last ten years of his life. Similarly, when Harry ran out of silk socks (the only kind he would wear) after the First World War, Win shopped all over London till she found in Hanover Square a little establishment specializing in small silk socks, mainly sold to Japanese. Win bought the entire available stock. When it began to run out she found that the Hanover Square establishment had disappeared; so it then occurred to her that boys of about twelve, from middle class families, wore silk socks to parties; and she tried Rowe's in Bond Street, which specialized in sailor suits and other items for the young. Thereafter this shop sent a tailor to measure Tich for his coats, suits, shirts and handmade footwear—from special lasts. (In the late 1950s, when his daughter had trouble in getting shoes to fit her, Win suggested trying Rowe's; but, on inquiry, they were disappointed. 'Oh, what a pity', said the manager, 'we've only recently disposed of Little Tich's lasts.')

From 1916 onwards Win settled, on her own, in a London flat. She did not take Harry's name, because they never lived openly together. She never visited him at his flat. When he visited her he always left before midnight and never stayed overnight. When they were able to go to a hotel together, separate bookings were always made. Never could they enjoy, she said, the ordinary human pleasure of a double room, openly shared.

One day, about eighteen months after their relationship had begun, they were out golfing together when Harry complained that he felt dreadfully sick. On several later occasions he again felt a spasm of violent nausea, which quickly passed away. He did not consult a doctor, as they agreed that it must be 'a touch of dyspepsia'. But then Win began to feel sick as well; and as this happened after a riding accident, when a horse bolted with her, Harry thought that although this, too, was probably just a touch of dyspepsia, Win had better see a doctor. To her astonishment the doctor told her, after examining her, that she was pregnant; what is more, she was *seven months* pregnant. Her period was habitually irregular, and she just hadn't noticed her condition. You can see why she was described on an earlier page as innocent and unsophisticated.

Win was due to meet Harry that day, to see a show together in London. She told him the news just before the curtain rose. They sat in numb silence, holding hands and staring blankly at the stage. At the first interval they left. Neither of them remembered afterwards what that first act was about, let alone what the show was called. What did occur to them was that Harry's sickness was an odd case of precognitive empathy, though they didn't put it in quite that way. Somehow he was able to identify with her problems, before she knew what they were; and, more than that, to identify with her physical condition.

From that moment Ivey Latimer's theatrical career was over. This delighted Harry: it had long been his belief that the stage was no place for a woman. She would now always be at home, waiting for him, permanently visitable up till 11 p.m.; and, very soon, his child would be there too. He arranged for Win to have the best medical care, paying for the services of the finest gynaecologist available. He insisted that everything possible should be done for her welfare. But for Win it was not so simple. She found it hard to accept 'forced retirement' and to confront the difficulties of being an unmarried mother, far more formidable sixty years ago than they are today. She was deeply upset that all her family, except for her father, virtually ostracized her: only

127

Mr Ivey came to see her after the birth. She was worried about Harry's reputation. What did his family think? What did they know? Were people talking? His refusal to discuss the subject did not lighten her anxiety. And she was lonely, for Harry could not be with her for much of the time. Never at night, he insisted. Not every day. Sometimes, when he was working out of London, she could not see him for weeks on end. She accepted the fact that he could not, *would* not, leave Julia; that she could not be his wife; but she lived under considerable nervous strain, much greater than either Harry or she realized.

When the moment of confinement came, Win was living under an assumed name at a flat in Bloomsbury. She was Mrs Winifred Emmerson, whose husband was 'abroad'. And on 23 February 1918 a baby girl, Mary Winifred, was born to Mrs Emmerson at 93 Ridgmount Gardens, a home (about half a mile from Bedford Square) which she left within a few weeks. It was an unusually difficult and painful birth: Win endured sixty-four hours of labour. Harry was working at Brighton. He got a telegram from Win's mother announcing the news just as he was going on for the first house. That night he wrote to her, addressing her as 'Beloved':

> So we have got our wish after all and it is a little girl. How I wish I could see you both, sweetheart mine, but I must be content with thinking of you. When you are strong enough to write, let me know all about it and what the little pet is like. How I wish I could see it. I am enclosing £20 and will send or bring more on my return from Brighton. Darling I send you my heart's best love and a million kisses and not forgetting some for 'little Mary'.

Harry's 'Beloved' was so weak and ill that she scarcely knew what 'the little pet' was like. Three weeks after Mary's birth she developed pleurisy. She was in no condition to cope with the baby, her nerves were in shreds, and she decided to let 'Little Mary' be looked after by a nurse in the country. This began a sad and nomadic year. First, Win went to stay with her parents in Hove to recuperate, alone—they wouldn't have taken her with her baby— but after a couple of unhappy weeks she fled from the family atmosphere and found a room in London, in a Gloucester Place boarding house-cum-private hotel. She stayed here until the proprietress began to show apparent signs of disapproval about the afternoon visits of Mr Relph, who frequently came to tea whenever he was in London. One day, returning from a short visit to see her baby in the country, Win found that the proprietress had—contrary to established arrangements—let her room go; an apparent accident which she saw as a deliberate exclusion. So Win had to move again. She was still on her own. A year after her birth, Mary was still in the country, although Win was missing her dreadfully and suffered from recurrent fits of violent weeping and bouts of loneliness and melancholia. It all seemed a long way from those midnight fireside chats in Liverpool between Hinbad and Sinbad.

A new life started, however, when Win told Harry that she wanted the baby with her, that she couldn't go on without her. Harry readily agreed; he was, no doubt, waiting for this to happen. They went to the country together to collect Mary and bring her back to London; and Win's health now began to pick up again, with her child beside her. The loneliness and depression disappeared. She regained the old self-confidence of her singing days. And, very soon, she found a new place to live. The Gloucester Place proprietress, Mrs Maud Holt, called to see Win; apologized for the previous misunderstanding; and asked 'Mrs Emmerson' to return to her hotel. In her nervous insecurity Win had clearly been misinterpreting Mrs Holt's behaviour. Now she was glad to agree to this proposal, if the right accommodation could be arranged for her child, a nanny and herself, and if it was understood that Mr Relph ('Uncle Harry') would be welcome to come for tea whenever he could find the time to do so. Everything was arranged. From then on the 'Emmersons' were at home at 64, Gloucester Place, which proved to be more of a home than the Hove house of Win's parents. They became close friends of Mrs Holt and her family (five daughters and a son). And Win learned a great deal from Maud: about catering; looking after children; managing on little money; and, not least, being resolute through all adversity. The lessons were to stand her in good stead.

Years later, Win said to her daughter, 'Of course, I little knew what it would entail for me, when I accepted Harry's proposal that we should be lovers. Some women think it's glamorous to be someone's mistress. It isn't. It's a damned lonely life. It's heartbreaking to see the one you love go back to another home, to be left uncertain always whether anything might happen to him—any time, any day. I'd be the last to know. Who'd have

129

told *me* if anything had happened to Harry? Who'd have sent for me if there was an accident?'

'A woman's a fool to become a man's mistress if she doesn't love him or if there's no real reason—for to a certain extent she loses something of her identity. And either way she is firmly branded by many people as immoral. To someone like me, cherishing your father's—well, his complete soul, and only him, for he'd been the only man in my life, that part was especially hurtful. I'm quite sure he never quite understood *how* hurtful, how I endured being a mistress and an unmarried mother. But then how could he? I never indicated to him the worrying and painful aspects of my situation, except in the smallest degree. It would only have added to his own troubles to think I was unhappy *because* of our relationship. And I suppose the irony was that we cherished one another more and more because of it. My prime concern was being of help to him, and taking his mind off his worries. It really didn't occur to me to think of marriage with him at any time.'

When Mary was two years old, there was another landmark in the relationship of her parents. Win talked one day to Harry about something she must have been considering for a long time: that it was a pity their child should not be generally known as his daughter, in due course, by taking his name. Harry had done nothing on this score until that moment, but he now readily agreed. Win was commissioned to discover how it could be done: how Mary Emmerson could become Mary Relph, short of Harry marrying Win, which was inconceivable. Win was officially informed that her child could bear her father's surname, if the father was willing to endorse the registration; so one day in 1920 Harry and Win went to Somerset House and returned with a new birth certificate for Mary. Win remained 'Mrs Emmerson', so in public Mary had still to be 'Mary Emmerson', in spite of the legal change in her name. Yet, nonetheless, this was for Win another demonstration that, in spite of Harry's absences and all the anomalies of her situation, his role in their lives seemed secure.

Mary, of course, knew nothing of these proceedings, or the ambiguities of her mother's status. All she knew was that when Uncle Harry came to tea he showered her with affection and with little gifts. As she could not quite pronounce his name this kindly visitor was, for some years, known as Uncle Ha'. For him,
130

Mary was 'The Cherub'. In every letter to Win after Mary's birth he always mentioned her by this nickname. He adored his daughter. She was a dream fulfilled, even though he could not see the dream as often as he would like. His happiness seemed to rejuvenate him. Although he was now over fifty, he was on top of his form. The punishing speciality of the Big Boots dance had been dropped, but many critics remarked on Little Tich's unflagging vitality and freshness. As one agent said, 'At his age he should be going right off now. But he's better than ever.' Harry survived the pressures of maintaining two households, one of them still ruinously expensive. Win conscientiously offered to give up the nanny and live in a simpler style than he had hitherto guaranteed; but, while gratefully recognizing her wish to help, he assured her that in any one year the upkeep of Win and Mary cost him a fraction of the bills in his official menage.

Win's life-style was comfortable, but it was lonely. Among her problems was the attitude of her family in Hove. Mr and Mrs Ivey were fond of Harry, and proud that Win knew such a celebrated artist. They were ready to give him hospitality, and to put up Win for a few days at any time. But although they finally submitted to their daughter's ultimatum—that unless she could bring Mary, she would never come to see them again—they found it very hard to give her daughter a proper welcome and full acceptance. This made Win all the angrier because her sister Liz had an illegitimate son, Jack, who was not only accepted by his grandparents but was brought up by them and took the family name. Liz had rejected Jack from his birth. Later she told him *never* to call her 'mother': an instruction for which he never forgave her. When Mary did visit the Iveys her grandparents were polite to her, but little more: no fuss was made, no presents were given, no games or outings were arranged. In spite of that she enjoyed her visits to Hove because of her cousin Jack (whom she assumed to be the Iveys' son) even though he played with her rather like a cat with a mouse, sometimes roughly, always mischievously. Unlike Mary, Jack was not strictly brought up. He was not always a good influence on her manners, by which Win and Harry set great store, so they tried to improve his behaviour and fill some of the gaps left by his doting grandparents, whose policy was one of *laisser faire*. In spite of this introduction to discipline, or because of it, Jack loved his aunt. Mrs Ivey said to

131

Win one day, 'I don't understand it. You're so strict with the children, yet Jack adores you. He even writes letters to your photograph, and throws them up as if for you to catch them.'

When Mary was about three, the nanny gave place to a governess. A succession of young women from various parts of Europe learned English from Win and Mary, while looking after the child's kindergarten schooling at home. It was about this time that home became a six-room flat in a block (Manor House) off the Marylebone Road, rented by Mrs Emmerson and paid for sub rosa by Mr Relph. The governesses had no domestic duties, and in turn they were company for Win on lonely evenings at those times—and there were many—when Harry was working out of London, or was at his official home with Julia. All of Mary's guardians spoke French, and were usually good needlewomen. Harry was delighted that, as his daughter grew older, she became bi-lingual. He was even more delighted that she showed an early aptitude for drawing. Encouraging her in every way he could, he taught her the rudiments of art. What he did *not* want to encourage was any idea of working in the theatre. Win agreed. Mary was taken to see her father at work, and sometimes to a children's show. She was also, at Harry's suggestion, given a few dancing lessons—'for deportment', he said—by Judith Espinosa, a distinguished dancer-teacher and sister of Edouard, a friend and admirer of Little Tich. But both Harry and Win were determined that, as the stage was 'no right life for a woman', they should do their best to insulate The Cherub from its appeal. They were all the more alarmed when, in spite of active dissuasion, Mary showed an increasing disposition to try somersaulting, acrobatics and walking on her hands, not to mention playing with her father's wigs. Harry was happier in fostering her interest in gardening, one of his dormant hobbies. As a member of the Royal Zoological Gardens Society, he rented a plot for Mary to work on in the Botanical Garden (later opened to the public as Queen Mary's Gardens). One year she won first prize there, but it was Harry who had done the real work.

By 1925, ten years after Harry and Win first met, he was free from many charges on his purse. Death had removed Harry Alaska, Roudy Knoepper, his stepbrother Will, his nephew Herbert (Georgiana's son) and other beneficiaries. Paul had disappeared. Yet Harry's financial problems were more serious than ever. It was not because of the cost of maintaining Win and

132

Mary: that, he insisted, was 'outside my real troubles'. The real troubles, he said, began with Julia. Having spent his capital reserves, as we saw in an earlier chapter, he had only his earnings to depend on. He was still at the top of his profession, but he was no longer always top of the bill. Tich was in his mid-fifties, and his profession was in the doldrums. His earnings dropped from £9750 in 1921/2 to £3743 in 1922/3. By 1924/5 they had risen again to over £6300, but dropped to less than £2200 in the following year. Because of the difficulty of getting the right dates at the right salary at home he had to work abroad increasingly to maintain his standard of living—or, rather, Julia's standard of living. When he explained his financial situation to her, he said, she seemed incapable of adjusting her life-style to reality. She wanted to continue to live at Bedford Court Mansions as she had always lived.

There was, it seems, little room for further economy in Harry's own life. He had cut his professional expenditure over the years, as is shown by the modest claims he submitted to the Inland Revenue. In 1924/5 he spent £100 on costumes, wigs, greasepaint, compared with £150 fourteen years earlier, in 1910/11; he cut his budget for both newspaper advertising and music from £100 to £50 (though in 1924/5 he paid £80 for 'songs and dialogues'); tips dropped from £75 to £46, though the dresser's annual wage was the same, at £130; and with fourteen weeks out of London, instead of eighteen, his estimated hotel bill was £140 rather than £180 (although a world war and a minor socio-economic revolution had intervened, it was still £10 a week). On the private side his personal regime had been relatively abstemious in food, drink and smoking for the past twenty years: this is no doubt one reason why he had scarcely ever been ill, and why in his late middle age he could still surprise audiences by his strength and *élan*. As he spent relatively little on his private pleasures (outside his secret family) he could not look for any material retrenchment there. But he had, somehow, to balance his budget. In this crisis he was immensely pleased when his favourite sister Agnes offered to help him. 'To think that out of all my family,' he said to Win, 'the only one who's never asked me to help financially is the only one to *offer* me help. Imagine, she's ready to put her entire savings at my disposal.' Agnes's entire savings amounted to just £25. And Harry did take them, without telling Win he had done so (in order not to make her even more alarmed

133

about his finances), although he repaid the loan very soon afterwards.

In this crisis—which was, it appears, rather worse than she realized—Win put forward a plan for economy: that they should give up renting the flat in Marylebone, and buy a small house through a building society. It would not only save money, but it would be a good investment: Harry owned no property of his own. It would cost him nothing initially, because she had a little money of her own that she would invest in it, enough for the initial deposit and the monthly payments, for the time being at least. Harry agreed, promising that he would take over the financial responsibility as soon as he could, preferably by outright purchase, and left it to Win to start house-hunting. She found just what they needed, she believed, in Brent, a district of North West London that still kept something of its rural past, though builders were rapidly filling in the green spaces. Win's choice was a show-house on a new estate, not yet completed, with unmade roads. It had four bedrooms, good gardenable land, and a garage; and although it was not far from schools, shops and an underground station, within easy reach of the centre, there were fields behind, a farm nearby, and a wide stream—the Brent, no less—running beside it. The price was £1475.

It took longer than 'Mrs Emmerson' expected to complete the purchase. To do so, she had to disclose her legal status. For un-married mothers to buy property today is still no easy feat: fifty years ago it was infinitely more difficult. But the fame of Little Tich (cited in confidence); Win's patent sincerity (and security); sympathy for her situation, for Harry's situation and (most im-probable of all) for the situation of the music hall apparently worked on the imagination of the building society officials, after persistent lobbying. Yet no word of this leaked into the press. Win and Mary moved in as soon as the roof was on: in September 1925. The new address was 93, Shirehall Park, Brent, Hendon. To Harry it held out the promise of a haven, if only for an occasional afternoon. And it was far away from Julia. Or so both Win and Harry believed.

Harry saw little of the new house or The Cherub that year. He was away much of the time in France, Belgium, Spain, Hungary and Germany. When he did manage to make a few fleeting visits, he was not told that Win was, for the first time, doing her own housework. She had started off with a cook-general from an
134

'exclusive' agency, but this lady was withdrawn from service when she reported that as Mr Emmerson was never in evidence and indeed, she suspected, did not exist, she thought it was not proper to work in such an establishment. So, for a long time, Win saved money by doing it all herself, with some help from Mary; all those petty and often penitential chores thought essential to good middle class housekeeping in the 1920's—tea-leafing the carpets; black-leading the grates; emery-papering the gas-stove and boiler; scrubbing the floor; lemon-juicing the brass-top table; cleaning and polishing the silver. It was all the harder that first winter because, as the new property had not yet fully dried out, the fires would not light easily and the house was damp and cold. But when Harry asked what had happened to the maid, Win told him she was away visiting a sick relation. He had, she felt, troubles enough of his own.

Strangely enough, Julia had come to the same hard necessity that year; though not, it seems, for long. One day on his return from a Continental engagement Harry was astonished to find her scrubbing the kitchen floor of the flat at Bedford Court Mansions, with her niece helping in the housework. She told him that expenses were higher than ever, higher than she had thought; there hadn't been enough money to pay the staff's wages; and the servants had all walked out. Harry declared that he had, as usual, provided Julia with enough cash for their pay; but in order 'to save a row' he gave her on the spot another cheque to cover her immediate needs and to get a cleaner in, adding that trying to do rough work was bad for her health. Julia had high blood pressure and a persistent bronchial cough—partly due to the English climate, said Harry, and rather more to her heavy smoking. She was suffering, too, from her anxieties about Harry and Win, anxieties that had by now been revealed to her adopted daughters, who later remembered their beloved Julia at this period as being often in tears because of 'that woman'. For them, as for Win, the faults in this marriage seemed to be all on one side.

13

MYSTERIES AND REVELATIONS

*Dozens of times I have run through Romeo's lines to myself until,
I am sure, I could play the part. Why should every stage lover be a
handsome man? Why should every clown be forced to be funny?*

Little Tich

Win's first winter in Shirehall Park was also Julia's last winter in
Bedford Court Mansions. One January morning in 1926 she was
found unconscious in the lavatory of number 79. The doctor
diagnosed cerebral thrombosis. Harry was there; Constance and
young Julia, too. Four days later Julia died without regaining con-
sciousness, on 7 January. Harry was at her bedside for much of the
time. He was in anguish. It was the first time that the girls had
seen *him* in tears. He was shocked and saddened by his wife's
sudden death. After nearly thirty years their strange and stormy
relationship was over. But the mysteries surrounding Julia and
Harry did not end with her death.

First of all, it seems that Harry had not recently been into Julia's
rooms. What he saw there disturbed and mystified him. He told
Win that much of her furniture and personal possessions had
vanished. It looked, Harry said, half-emptied, as if she had been
planning to move out. But where could she have gone—without
any money of her own? The servants walked out, saying they had
not been paid; and the girls 'disappeared', too (though they say
it was not until several days later that they left for France to stay
with Julia Récio's father, sent on their way by Harry with a piece
of his dead wife's jewellery for each). Harry was there in the big
flat on his own, for a couple of nights, with Julia's corpse. Then
he could stand it no longer. He rang Win to ask if he could stay
with her in their home. And although he had to make frequent
trips to the flat to settle matters of business he now became a
house guest at 93 Shirehall Park, where he moved into the spare
bedroom.

Returning to the flat before her funeral Harry was amazed to
discover, he told Win, that the partial removal had been com-

136

pleted: Julia's rooms had been stripped of virtually all their contents. Harry had already taken her street clothes—a Russian mink coat, with sable hat and muff; her handbag—made of solid gold mesh set with diamonds, and an emerald in the top framework; and the jewellery that she always carried in it, in a chamois-leather bag—a gold fob watch studded with seed pearls, a heavy gold chain bracelet strung with gold coins, and a number of rings. But the rest of her clothes, her make-up, her silver, china and glass, the whole luxurious surround of her life for the last thirty years, had gone. Her room contained her guitar, a pair of ebony castanets and a tortoiseshell manicure set. And that was virtually all that remained of Julia's domestic world; although Harry's own furniture and effects remained untouched and intact.

Harry had no clue, he told Win, to what had happened or who had done it. The porter at the flats could give no help. If any neighbours had noticed, and thought that this removal was strangely premature, then perhaps they thought that this was only to be expected from so strange a household. When he telephoned Win with the news Harry said, 'Come and see for yourself. Bring Mary, if you like,' adding with characteristic discretion, 'There's not a soul here.' Win came: it was the first time that she (and Mary) had seen Harry's official home. Whoever had organized the removal was clearly enough of a family intimate to know that Harry was now staying elsewhere. It gave him a curious sense of history repeating itself—with a difference; for it brought to mind the scene thirty years before in the Rue Lafayette when he found the Paris flat stripped of its contents and Laurie gone for good. But he did his best to make light of it to Win, with typical dryness. 'At least,' Harry said, 'it saves me a lot of bother getting rid of the stuff.'

There were greater surprises in store, said Harry, when he settled down to study Julia's papers. He discovered there—he did not tell Win how—that Julia was ten years older than he had always believed: not forty-eight (as her death certificate says) but fifty-eight. In other words, she was twenty-eight when they first met, not eighteen. Improbable as this revelation may seem without the evidence of Julia's birth certificate (which was, presumably, Harry's discovery) there is one fact which may support it. In an interview in 1901, Harry told a British reporter that when he had first met Julia three years earlier in 1898, she had been employed at the Olympia for ten years. Did she begin her dancing career at the age of eight? Harry himself had never questioned the fact.

137

The Olympia had, indeed, been open only seven years in 1897, so she would have begun at eleven. But, in fact, she was either *twenty* when they met in 1897 (after Laurie left him) according to her death certificate age; or, *if* they had met when she was eighteen, it had been some two years *before* Laurie went. Who can tell, now, what is the truth? Some readers may find it hard to accept that Julia could have carried off such a deception for thirty years. That was, in any case, what Harry believed he had discovered. It did not seem to disturb him unduly. 'Ah well, it hardly matters, does it?' he said to Win.

What did distress him was the discovery that for the past fifteen years his best friend Emile Footgers had been deceiving him with Julia. For much of that time she had not only been sleeping with him but keeping him, too. *That* was where the money had been going, it appeared. It was Emile's hypocrisy rather than Julia's in-fidelity that upset him. Shocked and hurt, Harry showed Win an unpaid bill for £600: it was the accumulated charge over several years for a room in the Finchley Road, rented to Julia. Most sur-prising of all for Harry, it was rented to her by Julia's foreign dressmaker, who had also been Laurie's dressmaker thirty years before. Madame X, who had a fashionable shop in the West End and a house in Hampstead, had become a personal friend of Julia's. Julia's niece had worked in her establishment for a time in order to make some pocket-money and contribute to her upkeep. Harry must have known of this relationship, and Madame X's bills must have figured prominently among Julia's financial burdens. But the echoing association with Laurie at that moment seemed remarkably eerie, in the light of the sudden, unexpected stripping of Julia's rooms, and the discovery of her double life. Harry paid Madame X's bill for the rented room, on Win's advice. 'Best be done with it and forget it,' she said. But she didn't forget it herself, not sur-prisingly. To her it seemed to point, in some way that perhaps nobody would ever be able to follow to the end, towards an ex-planation of the financial mysteries that Little Tich had tolerated with such strange stoicism for so many years. Had he been all the time, she wondered, under pressure—without realizing it—from a criminal conspiracy? Were both Laurie and Julia unwilling agents, through some bizarre underworld connection, of a black-mailer who had secretly milked Little Tich of a fortune? Was Julia herself blackmailed into complicity?

Yet if so, what was Harry Relph's secret? What had he done

138

that was worth blackmailing, and that he would hide for thirty years? And why should the conspiracy stop now, with Julia's death? Did he pay up all those years because he was frightened of threats to his life? He had at one period told Agnes that for this reason he was afraid to travel alone; though he usually did so in later years. It seems incredible that a wealthy international star should allow himself to be blackmailed for half his lifetime without calling for help from the police. Little Tich was a man of intense personal pride and conspicuous moral courage, with an acutely protective sense of his own dignity. Could he have borne so much humiliation for so long, without exposing his persecutors? According to Win, those who knew him intimately would say 'yes'. But though the conspiracy explanation is one that his daughter finds appealing, because she believes that Julia inveigled him into marriage and that Julia and Harry were *always* incompatible, it does not seem convincing to her collaborator in this book.

A more prosaic explanation is that Harry Relph was, indeed, blackmailed—by Julia, all alone. What she practised, consciously and/or unconsciously, was emotional blackmail: perhaps the most insidious kind of all, the kind that you can never pay off. He had once been captivated by her, both sexually and emotionally, before their marriage. He remained in bondage, unbreakably, long after he had ceased to love her or to need her. He was silent about that bondage, but he was incapable of escaping from it. He felt not only sorry for her but responsible for her, and he indicated that to Win. He could never marry her, he said, because Julia was a Catholic and would never give him a divorce; and made no pretence that he could ever leave Julia while she was alive, however willing Win might be to live together without marriage. Although he apparently never suspected Julia of having affairs with other men, the discovery at her death can scarcely have come to him as a great surprise—though the fact that Emile was her lover did astonish him. Moreover, he had never vilified Julia during his affair with Win, but had always spoken with understanding (if mystification) about her personal problems. And neither Harry nor Win talked unkindly about Julia then or afterwards: their daughter was brought up to regard the second Mrs Relph (whom she had never met) with respect and affection. At her death Harry went into deep mourning. So did Win. Heavy, black-deckled stationery was used. Mary was gently told by her mother that she was to be very quiet and not worry Uncle Ha'

139

with anything for a while, because his wife—'a most kind lady'—had died. There was no celebration at Shirehall Park, not even so much as a declaration to Win that he was glad to be free at last. But when he came back from Julia's funeral, he went on his knees to Win and begged her to marry him, avowing his profound love for her. His bondage to Julia was over; but it was not as an enemy or a conspirator that he mourned her.

In considering Harry Relph's financial crises in the 1920s, moreover, there is an additional fact to be borne in mind. As we have already observed, his income dropped very steeply in one year, 1922/3, by £6000; and in 1925/6 it dropped by over £4000 from the previous year to a record nadir of under £2200, compared with £9750 in 1921/2. Whatever the degree of Julia's unchallengeable responsibility for the drain on Harry's capital resources, such a brutally sudden slump in income was clearly a contributory cause for his sale of stock. Where else could the money come from, when the life-style in Bedford Court Mansions was virtually unchanged and when he himself had shouldered an additional charge on his earnings, however small was the cost of maintaining Win and Mary by comparison with that crowded and expensive household in Bloomsbury? Understandably, Harry was inclined in his own mind to exaggerate Julia's culpability, because of her ingrained habits of spending and her inability to adapt to changing circumstances; and he tended to look away self-protectively from the disheartening figures of his own declining earning-power, and to undervalue the major part that this played in his financial dilemmas. This was all the easier for him to overlook because it still seemed possible for him to double his income in a year, and because there was no real decline in his artistry or his international prestige. But his profession was suffering from prolonged depression; horizons were shrinking, and with them bank balances were evaporating.

And what about the mysterious removal? Perhaps the servants had helped themselves : while he was at the flat after Julia's death Harry watched them return and carry away baskets of linen. It was their right, they said : Madame had paid no wages for some time, and they were taking the linen in lieu. Harry let them go; but it is very doubtful that he would have done so without being reasonably satisfied that they had not already carried off more substantial items by way of compensation. Perhaps Emile Footgers contrived the removal : he had been an intimate of the family for
140

nearly twenty years, so this would have aroused no comment. And he may have moved the goods to a home of his own, which he shared intermittently with Julia, and which Julia paid for. Emile disappeared from Harry's life as soon as she died: we can find no record of what happened to him (he died in the early 1930s) or whether Harry and he were ever in touch after the event. And Harry never discovered the existence of Julia's second home, which astonishingly remained a secret for over thirty years.

Many years after his death his daughter Mary unearthed quite accidentally yet another dimension to the story of Harry, Julia, Win and Emile. This is the place to tell the story, though it happened long after the 1926 revelations of Julia's double life.

While Mary was walking her two dogs in Hendon Park in the 1960s they took a friendly interest in another dog being exercised, and in the usual way of dog-proprietors Mary and its owner got into conversation. The strange lady, it turned out, was convinced that—although Mary and she had never met—she had been to school with Little Tich's daughter, and that she had quite often been to Little Tich's house, where she had been entertained by Little Tich's wife. But the school was a convent in Golders Green that Mary had never attended. The house was one in a Golders Green street, where neither Harry nor Mary had ever lived. And the lady was convinced that Mary's name was Constance, if—as she claimed—she was Little Tich's daughter. When Mary did her best to explain that Tich had only one daughter, herself, that Constance was his grand-daughter, and that he had never lived in Golders Green, the lady found it hard to believe. 'Everyone at school *knew* that Constance was his daughter, and that Mrs Relph was his wife', she said. And there was no doubt about the identity of Mrs Relph: a 'Spanish-looking lady' who ran a stall at the school's annual garden party, and gave them some 'lovely teas' in the Golders Green house. A similar encounter and another letter from a pupil at the convent later led Mary to do some investigating in the neighbourhood. In the directories of the period she found that there was, indeed, a house in Golders Green under the name of Relph, which had been sold in 1926, the year of Julia's death. She found a local jeweller who had, earlier, pawned some trinkets for Julia, had bought a vase at the sale of the contents of such a house, and recalled the 'lovely stuff' he couldn't afford. Mary also discovered an auctioneer who remembered selling a house (and its contents) associated with Julia early in 1926,

141

though neither he nor the jeweller remembered anything about the other people involved in the sale. It seems probable that they would have remembered Little Tich; and it should be repeated, at this point, that his real name was little known among the general public—or, indeed, among many younger members of his profession, where he had always used the name of 'Harry Tich'.

When Mary discussed her discoveries with the Relph family, she and Win were astonished to find that Agnes—Harry's favourite sister—had known about a Golders Green house in his lifetime; that its interior was, in many ways, a replica of Julia's part of the flat in Bedford Court Mansions; but that she had never told her brother about this solution to the mystery of how Julia spent his money. *Why* did Agnes keep it a secret from him? In some ways, this seems the oddest fact about the whole odd story. Because, it was said, Harry was already suffering enough trouble: if she had told him even part of what she knew, it would make it even worse for him. Why, then, did she not tell him after Julia's death, so that he might have benefited from the sale of this property—as, inexplicably, he apparently didn't? Why didn't Agnes, or her daughter Doris, tell Win after *Harry's* death? Because, Doris explained, they didn't want to hurt Win's feelings.

The family picture revealed by these belated disclosures is, indeed, a strange one. One apparently obvious solution to its mysteries may well have occurred already to some readers; that Harry did in fact know about the Golders Green house (which is how Agnes knew); that he had acquiesced in Julia's double life, the second home, the transfer of property there, and Emile's role as lover; and that he was far too ashamed of this indulgence to tell Win—so that he made up the 'mystery' of the removal. This would explain the apparent mysteries: why Agnes and her daughter Doris never told Win; how it was possible for Julia to rent or buy a house, run it, and entertain people there without any word reaching Harry; how her part of the Bedford Court Mansions flat could be half-emptied without him noticing; how the sale of what was, in fact, Mrs Relph's house (and her effects) could be achieved in London without Mr Relph knowing anything about it or benefiting in any way from it. Yet though seemingly obvious, this 'solution' fails to explain why Harry should have gone quite so far in deliberately subsidizing Julia's wildest extravagance when his own fortunes were in such relative disrepair; why he would ever have agreed with Win to take the house in

142

Shirehall Park, which was no more than a mile away from the house in Golders Green; why he should have invented a farrago of lies to deceive Win, at a moment when the need for deception (if that had existed) was over. Moreover, this 'solution' fails to take account of the principal, if imponderable, factor in his character, as presented by his third wife and daughter: that he was a straightforward, truthful man, incapable of such an imposture.

So we are left with the bizarre picture of these two underground households in North London, less than a mile apart, totally unconscious of each other: in one, a husband secretly visiting his mistress and child; in the other, his wife secretly visiting her lover—and, with no child of her own, passing off her granddaughter as her daughter: both establishments paid for, ultimately, by the husband. In retrospect, it seems a natural subject for a comedy, or a Feydeau farce. But in this great comedian's life it would have been no laughing matter. The nearest that Harry ever got to the secret, it seems, was the following encounter, as described by him to Win one day in the early 1920s.

I say, Win, what do you think? A man came up to me the other day in the middle of London who I'd never seen before in my life. He insisted on shaking my hand and said how pleased he was to meet me at last. He'd lived next door to me for years and years, and every time he'd called I'd always been out or away. What a pleasure it was to see me after all this time, he said, shaking hands. Frankly, I didn't know what he was talking about, he gabbled so fast, and then—poof!—off he ran. Now, wasn't that funny? Madman, I suppose.

Win was not so sure. Because of that 'madman', she suspected for years that Julia had another home. She never told him her suspicions, 'in case it upset him or stirred up trouble. But I was right, of course. He never knew it, but I was right.'

On further research, the strange story becomes even more complicated: another house in the same area, within about a mile, was occupied by A. Footgers until 1926—the year of Julia's death. The coincidence is too striking to be ignored: that both the Relph concerned and the Footgers apparently disappeared from the district in the year that Julia died. Were there *two* Golders Green households in which Julia was involved?

Whatever the feelings in Win's heart at Harry's proposal of

F

143

marriage on the day of Julia's funeral, after years of self-abnegation and acquiescence in her role as mistress, she kept control of herself and counselled waiting a little longer—till July, perhaps, putting a conventional minimum distance between the end of one marriage and the beginning of another. Quite soon, a new era opened. Harry's finances seemed to be clear, for the first time in years. He could live on his salary and begin to save again. Win helped him to get his accounts straight and to live more economically. For the time being he stayed in the spare room, with his furniture in storage. All went on as before, until the current governess did not return from her holiday. When Win inquired at the agency, she found she was in the dark again. The agency told her that as Mr Emmerson was never on the premises and Mrs Emmerson appeared, indeed, to be a single lady, they could not permit one of their girls to go on working there. When she told Harry, he did not react in quite the way she had expected. He said, 'Well, if that's how it is, we'd better get married straight away.' And so they did, not long afterwards, by special licence—ten years after their first time together.

It happened on 10 April, 1926, with the minimum of publicity, at the Caxton Hall, Westminster. Win's parents were the only guests. Harry had attempted to sidestep the press. After the brief ceremony the foursome went to Frascati's for a quiet celebratory lunch, and that evening Little Tich continued his engagement at the Camberwell Palace. There was one wedding present—from the Brighton sportsman and hotelier, Harry Preston (later knighted), a friend and admirer of Little Tich. Mary had been sent away for a couple of days to friends in Wimbledon. When she came home her mother quietly explained the new family situation. Uncle Harry, said Win, had had a very sad life. He had, all along, been her very own daddy, but he could never say so—for reasons too difficult for Mary to understand, just yet. One of these reasons, however, was that a very important lady in Uncle Harry's life, called Mrs Relph, would not have understood, either; and as this lady was not always very well, Uncle Harry did not want to upset her. If Mary remembered, that was the lady who had died a little while ago, for whom Harry had worn black. Yes, Mary did remember; and she remembered going to see a big empty flat with a piano standing on the bare floor. So now, Win went on, everyone could know that it was *Daddy*, not Uncle Harry any more; that he had a little girl called Mary Relph, and *she* was that little

144

girl; and that he had a wife called Mrs Relph, and that was her mother's new name. *Nobody* was called Emmerson any more.

Mary did not worry about these revelations. She took to the switch of names with little hesitation. The next time she saw Harry she shyly greeted him with 'Hello, Daddy'; they kissed; and Uncle Harry disappeared for ever. Now she had a father, just like all her friends. It was a decided improvement.

14

THE NEW LIFE

Although we're some distance apart, love,
I always am thinking of thee,
And I'm longing oh! girl of my heart, love,
For the day when we sit down to tea
In the nice little room with my sweet girl,
And her dear smiling face close to mine;
Not thinking a bit what I eat, girl,
Tho' your cakes and your tea are divine.
It's then that I know that I've found, Win,
The love that I've looked for so long;
Such a great love as yours knows no bounds, Win,
So lasting, so steadfast and strong.

In such loving doggerel—'hoping it will "hand you a laugh" '—
the newly married Harry Relph, aged fifty-seven, wooed his wife
by post from Paris—and other European cities. Much of his first
year of his third marriage was spent, as so often, working abroad.
Their time together, as man and wife, was all too short.

When Harry did get home to Shirehall Park he spent much of
his time in the garden, with Win and Mary. He had it planted
with a screen of trees, for he wanted the utmost privacy. Win gave
him a small greenhouse. Preparations were made to build a big
conservatory alongside the house. He brought in landscape
gardeners to make full use of the picturesque possibilities of the
River Brent. Contractors delivered dozens of rose bushes, fuchsias,
begonias, azaleas, lavender, lilac and magnolia trees. He wanted an
instant garden, full of colour. There was no time to lose. He was
starting so late. It was his first garden since he left Clapham thirty
years earlier. When the first twenty trees arrived in their sapling
state, Harry was disappointed and saddened. 'Good gracious, I'll
be dead,' he said, 'before they're anything *like* trees.' He spent
many happy hours, also, working with Win on the house as well
as the garden. A room was built above the garage and turned into
146

Harry's sanctum, with his cello, his music, his golf clubs, his cuttings and his painting materials—just as he had gathered them round him in his den over the stables, thirty years before, at Clifton House.

That first summer of their marriage, Harry took Win abroad for the first time—and Mary, too. When an engagement at the Folies Bergère ended prematurely (after France went off the gold standard, and the management could not afford his salary) Harry decided that he and Win should make it a holiday, which they shared with their daughter, her governess and Jack Ivey at the Bristol. Among the memorable moments of that month's holiday for Win was the night at the theatre when Mistinguett on the stage called the attention of the audience to the presence of Little Tich, and made a presentation to him of a little statuette of himself in his big boots, while handing a long-stemmed red rose to Win. Later that year, in November, the three Relphs set out for Australia, where Harry had been invited to tour at £300 a week. He had decided to turn down an American offer of £400 a week, because it meant at least three performances a day—a physical strain, combined with the marathon travelling involved, of which he no longer felt himself to be capable. This Australian visit ended prematurely in Sydney, after humiliatingly boorish behaviour by the audience, throwing pennies on the stage. But in spite of that public ordeal, Harry enjoyed much private happiness on his journey across the world with his wife and daughter.

The Relphs got back to England in March. During the rest of that year they lived quietly at Shirehall Park, work permitting. Harry found the new family life too absorbing and delightful to be bothered with entertaining. He did not want 'other people' around: particularly, theatre people. When he was at home he shut off completely the world of the stage. Apart from his gardening, he still liked to paint; to play the cello (to himself and sometimes to his daughter); to have a game of golf (sometimes with a professional friend like George Robey); to see a show with Win, or dine out occasionally; to take Mary and Win to Richmond Park.

Financially, too, it was a new life. By the winter of 1927 Harry's financial position was straight. He had earned twice as much as in 1926 (in spite of the fiasco of the Australian trip). He had taken over payments on the house from Win, paid for the structural additions and the gardening programme, kept up to

147

date with tax, and he still had money in the bank. The following year he planned to pay off the balance of the house's purchase price in one lump sum. Everything was working out well.

Then it happened. During a two week engagement at the Alhambra in November 1927 he introduced a new number, 'The Charlady at the House of Commons', with a line in political patter. His costume was a hideous frock, a bedraggled apron and a scrag wig, and he carried a bucket and a mop—borrowed from home, because of its realistically 'used' look. One of Tich's bits of business was to flip the mop up into the air from the ground by standing on its fringed top; but on his first Wednesday this did not go as planned. The mop flew up, but it hit Tich a heavy blow on the back of his head. The audience thought it was all part of the act, and, although he was in pain, he played up to it and carried on. The pain subsided into a headache; then the headache disappeared. Only a slight bump and a sore place remained. He finished a very successful week apparently unaffected by the accident. On Sunday morning, in high spirits, Harry chatted to Win—in the neighbouring bathroom—from his bed before he got up for his bath. He said he was going to buy a car and have her taught to drive. He told her it was time she bought a new winter wardrobe of clothes. Win asked him, 'Shall I put your bath on when I've finished mine?' Harry didn't reply. She repeated the question. There was still no answer. Win found him with his head slumped forward. Little Tich had had a stroke. He never spoke again.

For three months he lay paralyzed in his right arm and leg, mute except for unintelligible murmurings. Upon medical advice Win stayed with him day and night. Only she could understand his signs and give him some comfort. Three consecutive specialists were called in. The third, Sir Alfred Fripp, diagnosed pernicious anaemia, which had been developing over many years; the thrombosis had been caused by the blow from the mop. Little Tich would never be the same again, said Sir Alfred, but there was a chance of partial recovery. It slowly became clear, however, that this chance was receding. At 6.26 on the morning of 10 February, 1928 Harry Relph and Little Tich died. He died without pain, looking as if the great contentment he had found in the last years of his life was his for ever.

Placards announcing the news of Little Tich's death brought one immediate result. Win was telephoned by Paul Relph, whom she had never met (she was three years his junior). 'I have just heard the dreadful news,' he said. 'Is there anything I can do? May I come to see you?' Shortly afterwards he arrived by taxi. Win asked him if he wanted to see his father, whom he had not met for years. He went alone up to the bedroom, where he stayed a long, long time. When Paul came down again to the dining-room, where Win was waiting, he stood looking silently at the fire. Then, leaning his head on the mantelshelf, he wept for many minutes. 'Poor father. Poor, poor father,' he said to Win. 'What a dreadful life he had! If only he had met you twenty-five years before he did, how different everything would have been.'

The funeral took place at the Marylebone Cemetery, in the East End Road, Finchley. It was a reunion of the Relph family: Harry's eldest brother, John; his eldest sister, Elizabeth Lee, with her son and daughter-in-law; Harry's favourite sister Agnes Williams, and her daughter Doris; and his brother Ted—half the Relphs who once upon a time had filled the rooms of the Blacksmith's Arms at Cudham. The Iveys were there, with Win's sister Liz and her husband. There were no Récios, or Constance, but Paul, her father, was there.

For Mary, now ten, he was one compensation in this unhappy time. She took an immediate fancy to her stepbrother (nearly thirty years her senior). On his side Paul declared how much he felt at home with Win and Mary; how, from now on, he was going to see a lot of them; how he was going to give Mary dancing lessons; how he would be back in a week or two. Off he went with some photographic mementoes of his father. They waited. And waited.

Paul did come back. But not until ten years later. Then, out of the blue, he telephoned one day to ask if he could have an old skip that had once belonged to his father, preserved in the Iveys' attic in Hove. He had guessed that Win could not throw away anything of Harry's. Win said, of course, that Paul could have it; and reminded him that he was always welcome at Shirehall Park. Paul was warm in his assurances: he would be in touch again soon. They waited. The next time was five years later, during the war. Paul suddenly reappeared at Shirehall Park, shabby, unshaven and virtually down and out. He had been bombed out of his Camden Town lodgings, losing all his belongings, he said, including mementoes of his father. But Paul was stubbornly independent: he would accept no kind of help, any more than he

149

would (he said) consider any kind of work but theatrical work. He left Win and Mary in high spirits, taking with him more souvenirs of Little Tich, promising to keep in touch. He never did. They never met again.

The date of Paul Relph's death was unknown to his daughter, his wife or his stepmother. It happened, we have discovered, twenty years after the death of his father—on 9 April, 1948, in an Islington hospital, of a stomach cancer. He was 58.

Harry Relph left no will. Although he did not, as some press reports suggested, die penniless, Win had to work hard for many years to maintain the house in which they had been so happy, and to make it yield an income for Mary's education and herself. In the late 1940s, with her daughter's help, she turned it into a small hotel. When it was sold in 1971, she had lived there for forty-six years: only two of them with Harry. It is now a Jewish eventide home. But it carries a blue plaque fixed by the GLC in 1968, a year after the centenary of his birth, inscribed:

Little Tich (Harry Relph) 1867–1928
Lived and Died Here

On his memorial stone in Marylebone Cemetery are these words:

In the World's Garden of Memories lives
The
Beloved Genius
LITTLE TICH
English Comedian. Dancer. Musician
Composer. Linguist. Artist
Né Harry Relph 21.7.1867–10.2.1928
Officier d'Académie
(Paris 1910)
'Le plus petit et le plus grand
comique du monde' (Paris 1928)

With the proceeds of the sale of the Shirehall Park house, Win and Mary bought a home in Brighton, where Win died two years later in 1973. Her health had steadily deteriorated after a massive heart attack in 1962. Yet in spite of several thromboses, bronchial pneumonia, two attacks of pleurisy, and a two year period of total blindness, she retained an uncanny youthfulness of face and spirit. She died happy in the knowledge that her beloved

Harry's story was being worked upon by Mary as a tribute from them both. On a memorial stone, beside his own are the words:

Also
His Beloved Wife
Win
(Ivey Latimer–Actress)
26.2.1892–17.12.1973
'Unconquerable Love'

Nearly forty years after his death, in 1964, his daughter Mary went up to the loft of their Shirehall Park home, at her mother's request, to search for some family papers. There, in dust-covered trunks, she discovered to her surprise a treasure trove of music hall history: programmes, music, contracts, letters, cuttings and photographs. She had never before read the world-wide reviews of her father's work. The Cherub suddenly saw the man who had been Uncle Harry in a new light. 'It made me feel as if I had just been introduced to a great personage. I wanted to tell the world about it. But I also felt as if I had met my own father again, and I had what I can only describe as a great inside shaking, in thinking of him with a renewed respect and a greater love.' That was the beginning, some fourteen years ago, of this book.

When Mary had spent many laborious months in research for a biography of her father, she came to the conclusion that he had never married Julia. She could find no record of any marriage in the family files, or in Somerset House, or anywhere else—and as Harry had been telling the press that Julia was his wife several years before they could have married (i.e. while Laurie was still alive) Mary concluded on this, and other apparent evidence, that the tie that had bound her father to Julia Récio was not a legal one. In the course of completing this book, it emerged that her conclusion was wrong: Julia's marriage certificate was in the possession of her nephew Fred in France. But the point of telling this story here is that neither Mary nor her mother thought the less of Harry for pretending, as they then believed, that he was married to Julia. When Mary asked Win whether she didn't think it had been dreadful of Harry not to marry her when he was legally free to do so, Win replied:

I can't possibly think the less of Harry, just because he wasn't married to Julia. It wouldn't have made any difference to our relationship if he'd told me in our first years. For really, when you come to think of it, he *wasn't* free: he was under her thumb so much. And in such a way, I suppose, that he thought it best for me—and for people generally—not to know the truth. Poor man, he suffered so much from the demands she made on him. If circumstances had been normal for him, and it had been just an ordinary tangled affair, he would have shed himself of her. He was quite capable of doing that. That I know. For all we know, he may have considered it a form of protecting me, as well as letting sleeping dogs lie. The more I think about it, Mary, the more I think what you have found out is the truth. But your father was under great strain, and my prime concern was being of help to him and taking his mind off his worries. I can honestly say that I never bore Julia any malice or jealous thoughts, although I knew she was the source of Harry's troubles. It didn't occur to me to think about marriage with him at any time, because he had told me it was out of the question. I didn't think like that. I *loved* him.

15

THE LITTLE GIANT

My recollection of my father is that he could make *anything* funny.
Today, whenever I laugh at a comedian, or a situation, or a joke
in somebody's act I can see again his sense of comedy, his idea
of the ridiculous, or the ridiculous truth of things. When I think
of all the leading professionals I have seen through the years it
is as if he is scattered amongst them—a bit of him in all that is
best in comedy.

Mary Tich

When Harry Relph died in 1928, the tributes to his comic mastery
as Little Tich—collected in a gilt-edged book by the Press Association and presented to his widow—confirmed that his unique
status in European music hall did not depend only upon his unique
stature. René Bizet went so far as to say that his death was possibly
the greatest loss that the music hall had ever suffered; for he was
one of the greatest, if not *the* greatest, of its comic artists. In the
half-century since his death his name has not been forgotten: it
may be found, briefly, in several books of reminiscences and in
all histories of the music hall and variety stage. Tich's career was
recalled by the BBC in a 1940 radio programme, in which his
widow played her real-life role; and, during the centenary of his
birth in 1967, by an interview with his daughter Mary. Four
years after that Anglia Television screened a film tribute to Tich.
He has been paid homage by J. B. Priestley, Sir Osbert and Sir
Sacheverell Sitwell, Jacques Tati, Sir Neville Cardus, Paul Nash
and others.

Yet, although Tich's name lives on, it is mainly as an idiomatic
tag for somebody who is unusually short. As an artist, one of the
greatest in music hall history, he has been somewhat neglected and
underrated. This is partly because of his own reticence and hatred
of publicity; partly because of his relative detachment from the
variety world; rather more because his success depended not so
much upon his songs as his dancing, not upon jokes but upon
personality, technique and charisma, not on being double-mean-

ingful but double-jointed; and most of all, perhaps, because of luck. All his life he was a soloist, a loner, an oddity; and although as an actor, acrobat, dancer and mime of irrefutably dramatic talent he could and did transcend his disabilities, he has had the misfortune to be remembered, if at all, for his 'very littleness', in the number which he most disliked and which he had abandoned some twelve years before his death. If Toulouse-Lautrec's picture of him had survived; if he had written or collaborated in his own autobiography, as Robey, Randall, Chevalier, Chirgwin, Dunville, George Mozart, and many lesser artists did; if his songs had caught the public ear as Billy Merson's or Harry Champion's or Charles Coburn's did; if he had been more widely recognized on this side of the Channel as one of Chaplin's early influences; if he had staked his claim to immortality in a few more reels of film—then Little Tich would have kept his place among the giant talents of international variety, in the music hall history of clowning and dancing. We hope that this book may put him back there, where he belonged for forty years, where he still belongs half a century after his death.

How did he reach that place at the summit in his lifetime? In the preceding chapters we have sketched Tich at work and discussed some aspects of his comic expertise. Here, in conclusion, we will try to summarize and enumerate the main elements in his success as an artist. And we will preface that attempt by defining some of the things Tich was *not*. He was neither a deadpan comic nor a daft one; neither a Norman Wisdom little man nor a Max Wall eccentric; neither a butt nor a Buttons (though he had the boyish, chirpy, natty look for that role in real life). He was not Cockney, or pseudo-posh, or mid-Atlantic. Although he could be and often was subtly suggestive, he was never blue. Nor was he sentimental, in his stage self or its many incarnations. He was not a gag-man : his jokes were perhaps the least important component of his act.

Moreover, although it is true that Tich exploited his lack of inches with persistent inventiveness throughout his career, that physical abnormality alone cannot account for his especial fame. Many other performers below normal height, often calling themselves Little this or that, appeared in American and European music halls, and some reached the principal stages, but few stayed the course : none, like Tich, topped the bill for nearly forty years. The fact is that to his admirers Tich's height became of

154

secondary importance. According to a *Guardian* critic in 1917, 'his humour does not depend upon an accident of physique; he would have been just as funny had he grown to the height of seven feet. He is possessed of a great comic genius—great not, perhaps, in its range, but in its intensity.' Or, to quote a *Morning Post* obituarist, 'he made every possible use of what to an average personality would have meant fatal disabilities, but at the same time there was about everything he said and did on the stage a virile force that made us occasionally forget these altogether.'

More positively, Little Tich was *funny to look at* : he had a Punchinello-like face, with a sly and rolling eye, unusual mobility of features, an expressive mouth and chin : a face that, like all true clowns' faces, spoke to the audience loud and clear (or soft and unmistakably) without the need of a word. When he did speak, he was *funny to listen to* : he had, as Paul Nash described it, 'a voice of many modulations from shrill girlish piping to guttural innuendoes and sibilant "doubles entendres" '; and he had the supreme felicity of that clownish benediction—an immensely, irresistibly infectious laugh, which helped him to exercise his sway (as Sacha Guitry said) over both the coarsest and the most cultivated members of his audience. When he moved, he was *funny to watch*—as an acrobat, a dancer and a mime (as we have already illustrated). As a Glasgow reviewer in 1916 commented : 'His every tone and gesture provoke laughter quite independent of the words he utters . . . Such comic genius gloweth where it listeth, and in the case of Little Tich it finds expression chiefly in gesture : a wave of his arm, a turn of his leg, a twist of his foot, and he can set the house in a roar.' Or, to quote another critic in 1915, 'he puts more meaning into a gesture or a grimace . . . than most entertainers put into a spoken part.' These gestures, said J. B. Priestley, were 'like little epigrams in a new language . . . so quick and neat, so energetic and intelligent.'

As Mr Priestley has also said,' he was really a very clever little man', and Harry Relph's *intelligence* was of prime significance in his career; for it was the kind of intelligence that comprised (instead of inhibiting) the instinctive wisdom of a performer-artist; quite apart from his ability (commented upon, even now, with unintentionally patronizing wonder) to speak four languages and discuss religion, mathematics and philosophy. As one Australian admirer later observed :

It is the brain behind the face which is the secret of his success. The little tricks that punctuate all his foolery, the constantly recurring bits of by play, the sudden changes of intonation, and the unexpected gestures and quaint steps of dancing, are all wonderful examples of the careful thinking-out which produces the art which conceals art. For at no time can Tich be noticed labouring at his fun; it is all apparently spontaneous, and bubbling with mirth, as the laughter of a child.

The combination of technical precision with apparent spontaneity, of artifice with improvisation, was one of Little Tich's gifts that made an especial impression upon Parisian observers. It enabled him to appear to London critics as 'fresh', 'wonderfully volatile' and 'surprisingly inventive' after thirty years at the top. 'There seems nothing calculated or methodical,' said a *Guardian* critic. 'It is like the uncontrollable effervescence of a spirit of fun made all the more active and explosive by its confinement within a narrow physical compass.' His effects seemed (to a Transvaal critic in 1908) to be achieved in 'the simplest and most natural way'. To quote another voice, 'It seems unnecessary for him to work for an effect; one would as soon think of Puck practising a part. And yet one knows that such perfection of fooling must be the result of hard work: so that truly Little Tich has reached the highest point any artist can reach; he has attained the effortlessness of effort.'

Michael Billington has distinguished two kinds of comic genius: 'the instinctively funny, sublunary performer who, by some quirk of nature, makes us laugh the moment he appears and the more calculating droll who works on us through artistic skill and finesse'. Little Tich combined both kinds of comic genius. With echoes of Puck and Punch around him, he seemed at times halfway between a puppet and a goblin, not so much a comedian as a spirit of mischief, 'elfin and bizarre'. The *Manchester Guardian* obituarist, indeed, declared that he 'never portrayed normal human beings': all his characters had 'a quartering of elfland on the shield'. Yet, with all this, was combined the master-technician, whose 'perfection of timing'—said James Agate in *Ego 5*—was still impeccable at the very end of his career.

Like many clowns of the first rank, Little Tich developed a special relationship with the audience through his relationship
156

with objects, things and clothes: in the way, for instance, that—as a debutante—he made his train turn into a muffler, or a rug; or made it stick, immovably, to his tiny body, tripping him up and causing all kinds of embarrassments, so that his face reddened, his fists clenched and a miniature tempest of anger blew up, suddenly dissolving into a 'most delicious smile'. Tich made a great deal out of his hats: his straw boater, for example, which seemed to be 'enchanted' as it wobbled uneasily on his head, somehow rolled down his arm and then returned to its proper place; then fell to the stage, 'only to be taken at the very ultimate moment' by a foot or a cane and flicked into the air, to settle again on his head. Or, with the aid of his cane, he could make the little round felt hat he wore in his 'Johnny Green' number spin slowly in a circle on its edge around him; or he could make it move away from him, while trying to pick it up. Whatever he did, he made it appear that there was a reason for it, that it arose from some incident in the action of the character, and was not simply a routine or a show-off speciality.

Another element in Little Tich's success was his appearance of demonic energy, sustained until the end of his career. All his characters, said J. B. Priestley, seemed like 'visitors from a society of gnomes, and you began laughing at the first sight of them, all the more because they looked intensely serious, often arriving in a furious state of indignation.

The tale of his grievances was illustrated by nothing less than a fury of movement and gestures, The energy of these minuscule characters, these infuriated and maddening gnomes, was astounding. It made you feel you had spent your life as a mere languorous and supine giant. He seemed to fill the stage with people like you, unable to face his burning indignation and furious gestures . . . If he said he would show us what he thought about some obstreperous fellow, his dumbshow would almost explode into wild careering round the stage, punching and kicking away, defying men of any weight to come near him. If, as it frequently happened, things themselves were hostile and got him all tangled up, he would release for himself and for us the raising fury of the human spirit dragged down into such a world as this. Even without opposition his own wild eloquence, his determination to make a sensible point in a daft world, would carry him away, so that as a barrister he not only

157

thumped the table with his fist but also with his foot. There has never been such wildly energetic miming as this fiery little gnome showed us.

This 'fury' was, no doubt, fuelled by Tich's off-stage sense of grievance, the bottled-up aggression that made him long to batter down so many of the big people who looked down on him and talked down to him although, as he very well knew, he was far, far more intelligent, sensitive and *rich* than most of them. And it was this inner aggression that lent the quality of malevolence on which so many Parisian observers commented in his early career: the sense of *danger* which is, perhaps, indispensable to all top-rank performers in the near-genius class (from Kean to Olivier, from Grimaldi to Grock): the aura that made Sacheverell Sitwell describe Tich as a 'slightly horrific genius in his kind'.

There was, moreover, another dimension to his act, in which, as Priestley says, the audience 'observed and estimated it with him . . . He would suddenly take us behind the scenes with him, doing it with a single remark. He would drop a hat and be unable to pick it up, because he kicked it out of reach every time, and then mutter, half in despair, "Comic business with chapeau." ' In Paris he would murmur, 'Business avec accessoires', or 'Oh, *very* comic.' When juggling, he would say, in a prefatory aside, 'Very difficult.' Then, having tried and failed, tried again and failed again, he said, quickly, '*Too* difficult.' Or, having brought the house down at the Palladium with a bit of business, instead of repeating it for all it was worth, he remarked in a reflective aside, 'That's about enough of that, I think.' Writing shortly after his death, Priestley said: 'I think that was the innermost secret of this little droll's appeal. In the antics of this gargoyle there was all the time the suggestion of a companion spirit winking and nodding and shrugging at you over the crazy jumble and tangle of things.' In 1975 Mr Priestley added: 'what I didn't say then, because it was so obvious, I will say now. Little Tich was a really great comedian, a star of the first magnitude for ever twinkling.'

BIBLIOGRAPHY

Adhémar, Jean, *Toulouse-Lautrec. His Complete Lithographs and Drypoints,* 1965

Archer, William, *The Theatrical World of 1896,* 1897

Bailey 11, Joseph A., *Disproportionate Short Stature,* 1973

Beerbohm, Max, *Around Theatres,* 1953; *More Theatres,* 1969; *Last Theatres,* 1970

Behrman, S. N., *Conversations with Max,* 1960

Boardman, W. H., *Vaudeville Days,* 1935

Bodin, Walter and Hershey, B., *The World of Midgets,* 1935

Bost, Pierre, *Le Cirque et le Music Hall,* 1931

Busby, Roy, *British Music Hall, An Illustrated Who's Who from 1850 to the Present Day,* 1976

Calthrop, Dion Clayton, *Music Hall Nights,* 1925

Cheshire, D. F., *Music Hall in Britain,* 1974

Coborn, Charles, *The Man Who Broke the Bank,* 1928

Cochran, Charles B., *A Showman Looks On,* 1945

Courtneidge, Cicely, *Cicely,* 1953

Disher, M. Willson, *Clowns and Pantomimes,* 1925
 Winkles and Champagne, 1938

Dunville, T. E., *Autobiography of an Eccentric Comedian,* 1912

Espinosa, E., *And Then He Danced,* 1947

Ferguson, Sir Louis, *Old Time Music Hall Comedians,* 1949

Fisher, John, *Funny Way to be a Hero,* 1973

Gilbert, Douglas, *American Vaudeville,* 1940

Harding, James, *Sacha Guitry,* 1968

Hibbert, H. G., *Fifty Years of a Londoner's Life,* 1916

Honri, Peter, *Working the Halls,* 1973

Howard, Diana, *London Theatres and Music Halls 1850-1950,* 1970

Jacob, Naomi, *Our Marie,* 1952
 Me. 1933
 Me Over There, 1967

Jacques-Charles, *Cent Ans de Music-Hall,* 1956

Knowles, R. G., *A Modern Columbus,* 1915

Le Roy, George, *Music Hall Stars of the Nineties,* 1952

Lorrain, Jean, *Poussières de Paris,* 1902

Mackay, William, *Bohemian Days in London,* 1913
MacQueen-Pope, W., *The Melodies Linger On,* 1950
Mander, Raymond and Mitchenson, Joe, *British Music Hall,* 1965
Mistinguett, *Toute ma Vie*
Nash, Paul, *Outline,* 1949
Newton, H. Chance, *Idols of the Halls,* 1928
Priestley, J. B., *Particular Pleasures,* 1975
Randall, Harry, *Harry Randall, Old Time Comedian,* 1931
Reeve, Ada, *Take it for a Fact,* 1954
Rémy, Tristan, *Les Clowns,* 1945
Renard, Jules, *Journal de Jules Renard 1887-1910,* ed. Gilbert Sigaux,
   1960
Roberts, Arthur, *Fifty Years of Spoof,* 1927
Robey, George, *Looking Back on Life,* 1933
Rudorff, Raymond, *La Belle Epoque,* 1972
Scott, Harold, *The Early Doors,* 1946
Sherek, Henry, *Not in Front of the Children,* 1959
Sitwell, Sir Osbert, *The Scarlet Tree,* 1946
Sitwell, Sir Sacheverell, *For Want of the Golden City,* 1973
Stuart, C. D., and Park, A. J., *The Variety Stage,* 1895
Tich, Little, *Little Tich,* 1911
Tilley, Vesta, *Recollections,* 1934
Van Ash, Gay and Rohmer, Elizabeth, *Master of Villainy,* 1973
Verne, Maurice, *Musées de Volupté*
Williams, Bransby, *By Himself,* 1954
Wood, J. Hickory, *Dan Leno,* 1905
Wood, 'Wee' Georgie, *I Had to be 'Wee.'* 1948

POSTSCRIPT

Our thanks are due, abundantly, to many people who have helped in many different ways to make this book, by passing on recollections on Little Tich at work and Harry Relph in private; by making possible further researches in libraries and archives in Britain, France and America; by answering the authors' questions and drawing their attention to all kinds of material, often fragmentary and contradictory, that has gone into the creation of this portrait. Some of our witnesses noted below are no longer alive, for it is more than a dozen years since Mary Powell began work, single-handed, on a book about her father, and half a century since he made his last appearance on the stage. We cannot itemize here the help that each of them has given, and we have decided to exclude from the text a full annotation of sources, which often cannot be identified in detail. In outlining Harry Relph's private life, in particular, we have striven to present a balanced portrait; but we recognize that this may not satisfy some of our witnesses, particularly those who have kept devoted memories of his second wife, Julia; and, as we have emphasized in the text, there are many mysteries in the story and gaps in the record.

The prime source of this book has been the rich collection of material—cuttings, photographs, letters, drawings, music and other memorabilia—passed on by Harry's third wife, Winifred E. Relph, to their daughter Mary. We have drawn on the notes made by Mrs Relph about Harry's conversational reminiscences, and on the recollections of many members of the Relph family, past and present: notably, Agnes Williams (Harry's sister) her children Doris Williams, Ethel Williams, Minnie Carter and Harry Williams and her grand-daughter Pamela Light; Joan Lungley, Phyllis Walker and Leslie Rhodes, grand-daughters of Harry's sister, Elizabeth; Frédéric and Lita Récio, Julia Relph's nephew and niece; Constance Davies, Harry's granddaughter; and Olive Ivey (Winifred Relph's aunt); although we should like to make clear that they are in no way responsible for the picture we present here, for the first time.

Our thanks are also due to Sir Sacheverell Sitwell; Sir Ralph Richardson; Sir Norman Joseph; Richard Goolden; Don Ross; Bert Ross; Dr Hannah Winter; Dame Cicely Courtneidge; Evelyn Laye;

161

Harry Tate, Junior; Peter Honri; 'Wee' Georgie Wood; Ellis Ashton; R. V. Marquis; Michael Pointon; Raymond Mander and Joe Mitchenson; Charles Chilton; Grace Kinnibrugh; Doris Bates; Kathleen Kempner; Babs Henty; Barbara Holt; Dorothy Worledge; Mary Morton-Farris; W. F. Proudfoot; Joanne Walker; F. J. Collins; F. Corfield; Lester Martin; George Marshall; the Rev. Alfred C. Ford (Fawkham); the Rev. Bryan Isaac and the Rev. I. Leakey (Cudham); the Rev. Dennis Sweetman (Eynsford); the Rev. I. A. Hardaker (Chatham); the Rev. Donald Sherriff (St Paul's Cray); the Rev. D. G. Thomas (Darenth); the Rev. R. G. Tremellin (Southwick); the Rev. D. Wells (Farnborough); the Rev. S. C. Clark (Crockenhill); E. J. Barrett (County Clerk, Cook County, Illinois); W. J. Smith (Head Archivist G.L.C.); Frank Cole (Director of Libraries and Arts, Camden); Colin Bray (Courage's); Susan Lambert (Victoria and Albert Museum); Mlle. G. Volle (Musée Toulouse-Lautrec, Albi); Michèle Thomas (Bibliothèque Nationale, Paris); Louise Pacholik (Chicago Historical Society); G. Fordham (Divisional Librarian, Chatham); Janet Smith (Liverpool Record Office); Walter T. W. Woods (Divisional Librarian, Gravesend); Heather Dobson (Divisional Reference Librarian, Sevenoaks); Barry Totterdell (Borough Librarian, Brent); Derek Lewis (BBC Gramophone Librarian); John McKeown (Eccentric Club); to the staffs of the British Library, the British Theatre Museum, the British Film Institute, the British Institute of Recorded Sound, the London Library, the Guildhall Library, the Hendon, Brighton and Hove reference libraries, and the St Martin's Street branch of Westminster Libraries; and to Jennifer Belle, for her hospitality and assistance in Paris and to Peter Honri, for reading the proofs.

For permission to quote at some length from copyright material our thanks are due to J. B. Priestley and Messrs Heinemann, for extracts from *Particular Pleasures;* to the executors of Paul Nash and Messrs Faber & Faber, for extracts from *Outline;* to James Dillon White and Messrs Heinemann, for extracts from *Born to Star;* to the executors of S. N. Behrman and A. M. Heath, for extracts from *Conversations with Max,* published by Hamish Hamilton; and to other authors whose books are briefly cited in the text and identified in the booklist. Our illustrations are all drawn from Winifred Relph's collection, with the exception of the photograph of Paul Relph and his daughter Constance —to whom we record our thanks.

INDEX

163

164